A DAY IN AN AMISH KITCHEN

INTRODUCTION

THE simple, family-centered lifestyle of the Amish is especially appealing in these hectic times. And a perfect place to experience the pleasures of plain living is in the heart of any Amish home—the kitchen.

As everyone knows, most Amish cooks rely on wood- or propane-fired stoves and nonelectric ice boxes. Even so, their families still enjoy dishes like pizza or tacos, as you'll see in this unusual book.

In fact, you may be a bit surprised as you peruse the recipes that follow—many of the dishes are not what you'd expect to find in an "authentic" Amish cafe during a visit to an Amish settlement.

That's because these recipes are not tailored for tourists—they're family favorites directly from the kitchens of Amish cooks in 22 states and Canada.

In order to preserve the "flavor" of the originals, the recipes in this book are transcribed directly from the contributors' handwritten notes. Just reading them will give you a fascinating look at the culinary skills of Amish cooks.

If you should choose to try some of these recipes in your own kitchen, there are several things to bear in mind: (1) Most fresh ingredients, including vegetables, eggs, poultry and meats, are grown or raised right on Amish farms and may vary in size and quality from store-bought counterparts. (2) References to canned soups, fruits or meats often (but not always) mean *home*-canned.

(3) Instructions are simple and conversational and may include additional ingredients not listed in the recipe. (4) Cooking times and temperatures are for wood- or propane-fired stoves and may vary with gas or electric stoves.

In addition to recipes, you'll find plenty of colorful photos—many taken in Amish kitchens by the cooks themselves—plus lots of "kitchen chat". As you turn the pages, you'll feel as if you're right *there* with the "Plain People" as they prepare meals for their families. Enjoy! —*Bob Ottum, Editor*

CONTENTS

SOUPS, SALADS AND SIDE DISHES
6

BREADS AND SPREADS
12

MAIN DISHES
22

PIES
44

DESSERTS
52

COOKIES
72

CONDIMENTS
82

MAUDIE'S KITCHEN
86

Editor: Bob Ottum
Art Director: Julie Wagner
Photo Coordination: Trudi Bellin
Production: Judy Pope

© 1995 Reiman Publications, L.P.
5400 S. 60th St., Greendale WI 53129
International Standard Book Number: 0-89821-147-6
Library of Congress Catalog Card Number: 95-69388
All rights reserved. Printed in U.S.A.

Cover, page 3 photos by Bill Hentosh
Page 4 photo by Ronald N. Wilson
Back cover photo by John L. Randolph

For additional copies of this book or information on
other books, write: Country Books, P.O. Box 990,
Greendale WI 53129. Credit card orders
call toll-free 1-800/558-1013.

Sherry Pardee

Soups, Salads and Side Dishes

One-Gallon Potato Salad

4-1/2 lbs. potatoes boiled and shoestringed
  12 eggs, hard boiled
   2 cups chopped celery
 1/2 medium onion, chopped

Dressing

   3 cups salad dressing
 1/4 cup vinegar
 1/2 cup milk
   3 teaspoons mustard
1-1/2 cups sugar
   4 teaspoons salt

—Leota Burkholder, Goshen IN

Ribbon Salad

Layer One

   1 box orange Jell-O

Prepare according to directions. Pour into 8 x 8 cake pan and leave it set.

Layer Two

   1 small can crushed pineapple
  16 marshmallows
 2/3 cup milk
   1 8 oz. cream cheese
   1 box lemon Jell-O
   1 cup whipping cream
 2/3 cup chopped nuts

Heat milk, marshmallows and cheese in double boiler until melted. Add lemon Jell-O and stir until dissolved. Cool until partly set. Add pineapple, nuts and whipped cream and pour over first layer.

Layer Three

   1 box orange Jell-O

Prepare and put on top. Let set.

—Mary Beachy, Baltic OH

Cottage Cheese Salad

   2 boxes Jell-O
   2 cups boiling water
   1 cup whipped cream
   1 cup miniature marshmallows
   1 can crushed pineapple
   1 lb. cottage cheese

Mix Jell-O and boiling water. When it starts to thicken, fold in cream, marshmallows, pineapple and cottage cheese.

—Esther Borntrager
Curryville MO

Layer Salad

Lettuce
Cauliflower
Bacon bits
   1 jar mayonnaise
   1 tablespoon mustard
   1 cup white sugar
   3 tablespoons sour cream
Onion powder
 1/2 cup cream or milk
   1 pack Ritz crackers, broken
Shredded cheese

Put a layer of lettuce in bottom of a cake pan. Add a layer of cauliflower and bacon bits. Mix together mayonnaise, mustard, sugar, sour cream, onion powder and cream. Add a layer of this on top of above mixture. (The mayonnaise mixture is enough for 3 or 4 pans.) Then add a layer of Ritz crackers and a layer of shredded cheese.

—Susie Gingerich, Utica MN

♦ KITCHEN CHAT ♦

WE STILL HAVE a lot of garden goodies, which makes meal planning easier. The oak leaf lettuce is so good and tender yet. What would we do without a garden?

I dug my sweet potatoes Saturday. My sister told me her daughter dug one that weighed 9 pounds, 2 ounces. Remarkable. Our daughter Leah picked a couple tomatoes weighing 1-1/2 and 2 pounds.

The weather was so nice for us, with plenty of rain. But we're sorry for the ones who suffered in flooded areas. Much to be thankful for, and do we appreciate it enough?

We still have carrots, cabbage, lettuce, hot peppers, tomatoes, red beets, Chinese cabbage, winter radishes and endive in the garden. We will miss it once a killing frost comes.

—Elizabeth Coblentz, Geneva, Indiana

3-Layer Salad

Layer One

    2 boxes Jell-O (1 lemon, 1 lime)
3-3/4 cups hot water
    1 cup crushed pineapple, drained

Dissolve Jell-O in hot water. Stir in pineapple and let cool until firm.

Layer Two

    1 large pkg. cream cheese (8 oz.)
    1 cup whipped cream

Sweeten whipped cream with cheese and spread on top of first layer.

Layer Three

    1 cup sugar
    2 tablespoons flour
    2 eggs
    1 cup pineapple juice

Cook until thick. Put on top when ready to serve.
                    —Katie Hochsteller, LaGrange IN

Parslied Chicken Chowder

    2 tablespoons butter
    1/4 cup chopped onion
    1-1/2 cups cooked cubed chicken
    1-1/2 cups pared cubed potatoes
    1-1/2 cups pared cubed carrots
    2 chicken bouillon cubes
    1 teaspoon salt
    1/8 teaspoon pepper
    2 cups water
    3 tablespoons flour
2-1/2 cups milk
Fresh parsley, chopped

Melt butter in a 3-quart saucepan. Add onion and saute until tender. Add chicken, potatoes, carrots, bouillon cubes, salt, pepper and water. Cover and simmer 20 minutes or until vegetables are tender. Combine flour and 1/2 cup of milk in a jar. Cover and shake until blended. Add flour mixture and remaining 2 cups of milk to vegetables. Cook over medium heat, stirring constantly, until mixture thickens. Sprinkle with parsley. Makes 1-3/4 quarts.   —Mary Hersberger, Baltic OH

Good Scalloped Potatoes

    6 tablespoons butter *or* margarine
    6 tablespoons flour
    1 teaspoon salt
Dash of pepper
  1-1/2 cups milk
  1-1/2 cups water
    2 cups Velveeta cheese grated
    8 cups cooked and diced potatoes
    3 cups diced ham
    1 cup bread crumbs
    4 tablespoons margarine

Melt butter in saucepan; remove from heat. Blend in flour, salt and pepper. Gradually stir in milk and water. Cook over medium heat, stirring until thickened. Add cheese; continue cooking and stirring until cheese is melted. Fry bread crumbs in the 4 tablespoons of margarine and put on top of potatoes which have been mixed with rest of ingredients. Bake uncovered for 30 minutes in 350° oven.
—*Esther Miller, Millersburg OH*

Potluck Potatoes

    2 lbs. potatoes
    1/2 cup onion chopped
    2 cups Velveeta cheese
    1/2 teaspoon pepper
    1 can cream of chicken soup
    1/2 cup butter
    1 pint sour cream
    1 teaspoon salt
    2 cups corn flakes crushed
    1/4 cup butter

Dice potatoes. Cook until almost soft. Mix rest of ingredients and add to potatoes. Pour in a greased 5 quart casserole. Cover with crushed corn flakes mixed with 1/4 cup butter. Bake uncovered at 350° for 45 minutes.   —*Clara Weaver, Dundee OH*

> ◆ KITCHEN CHAT ◆
> ALREADY suppertime—what shall I get? Well, I have some leftover chicken and broth, so I make chicken noodle soup, plus a salad of fresh garden vegetables including celery, tomatoes, cabbage and a few snips of sweet pepper. Dessert is grape sauce served like a pudding.
> —*Mary Hostetler, Dry Run, Pennsylvania*

Chicken Dressing

    3 eggs
    1 cup chicken broth
    2 cups milk
    1 cup diced chicken
    1 onion chopped
    1/4 cup celery leaves
  1-1/2 teaspoon salt
  1-1/4 teaspoon pepper or less
    2 quarts bread crumbs (butter bread if desired)

Beat eggs, chicken broth and milk. Add chicken, onion, celery leaves, salt, pepper and bread crumbs. Bake with chicken or turkey or separate at 350° for 1-1/2 hours. If knife inserted comes out clean, it is done.   —*Leota Burkholder Goshen IN*

Potato Salad

    12 cups potatoes
    12 eggs, hard boiled
    1/2 medium onion, chopped
  1-1/2 cups chopped celery

Dressing

    3 cups salad dressing
    6 tablespoons mustard
    2 teaspoons salt
  2-1/2 cups white sugar
    1/4 cup vinegar
    1/2 cup milk

Cook potatoes until almost soft, then put through salad master. Mix first four ingredients. Blend the dressing ingredients together and add to the vegetables. Mix well.   —*Mary Yoder, Millersburg OH*

David Troyer

Parmesan Potatoes

    6 **large potatoes**
 1/4 **cup flour, sifted**
 1/4 **cup grated Parmesan cheese**
Salt and pepper as desired
Butter

Pare potatoes; cut lengthwise into quarters. Combine flour, cheese, salt and pepper in plastic bag. Wet potatoes thoroughly. Coat by shaking a few at a time in bag. Place in cake pan with 1/4 to 1/2 cup melted butter on bottom. Bake until golden brown at 375°. *—Barbara Schwartz, Geneva IN*

Overnight Potato Salad

  12 **cups shredded potatoes**
  12 **eggs, shredded**
1-1/2 **cups onion**
1-1/2 **cups celery**
   3 **cups salad dressing**
   3 **tablespoons mustard**
   3 **tablespoons vinegar**
1-3/4 **cups sugar**
   4 **teaspoons salt**

Cook potatoes until almost done, but still firm. Red potatoes are best. Chill in refrigerator. Shred chilled potatoes and eggs with a shoestring potato shredder (rather than cube) and mix well. Add celery and onions. Mix remaining ingredients in a bowl and pour over potatoes. Mix well. Let set overnight for flavors to blend. Chilling of the potatoes, especially if they are not red potatoes, is the secret to this recipe. If not chilled, they will crumble instead of shredding into long firm strands, which gives the salad its character.   *—Salome Miller*
Windsor OH

Garden Salad

    1 **large lime Jell-O**
 3/4 **cup water, boiling**
 3/4 **cup chopped green pepper**
    1 **small onion, chopped**
1-1/2 **cups chopped celery**
1-1/2 **cups chopped carrots**
    1 **large cottage cheese (small curd)**
1-1/2 **cups salad dressing**
    1 **cup Cool Whip**

Mix Jell-O with water and let cool. Mix chopped vegetables with cottage cheese. Add salad dressing and cool whip. Then pour Jell-O over this and fold in until well mixed. Turn into mold if you wish or a bowl with a tight-fitting lid.
—Kathy Ann Hershberger, Gonzales TX

Apple Salad

    1 **egg, beaten**
    1 **cup sugar**
    2 **tablespoons flour (rounded)**
    1 **pint water**
    2 **tablespoons vinegar**
Butter size of a walnut
    1 **teaspoon vanilla**
Apples, diced
Pineapple
Bananas
Marshmallows
Nuts chopped

Mix eggs, sugar, flour, water and vinegar. Boil until thickened. Add butter and vanilla. Add the sauce to apples, nuts, marshmallows, pineapple and bananas. Use desired amounts of fruit.
—Effie Troyer, Dover DE

◆ KITCHEN CHAT ◆

TODAY David Jr., age 15, helped me clean, sort, bag and weigh the potatoes we dug last Friday.

We were pleased with our yield this year—nearly 1,000 pounds from 50 pounds of seed. Some of the biggest potatoes weighed 2 pounds.

I'll can the small ones today. After I finish with laundry, I'll throw the small potatoes in the washing machine along with an old towel. They come out sparkling and ready for the jars.

—Emma Troyer, Williamsfield, Ohio

Pineapple Cheese Salad

- 1 pkg. gelatin
- 1 pkg. lemon Jell-O
- 1 cup boiling water
- 1/2 cup sugar
- 1 cup crushed pineapple
- 1 large cream cheese
- 1 can evaporated milk

Crumbs

- 1 stick margarine
- 3 cups graham crackers

Melt gelatin, Jell-O and sugar in water, cool until slightly thickened. Mash cheese and mix with pineapple juice. Beat icy cold milk to form peaks. Add other ingredients and pour on half of crumbs. Put rest of crumbs on top.　　*—Fanny Stoltzfus Rebersburg PA*

Tramp Soup

- 1 tablespoon ham base
- 1 lb. country smoked sausage (fried) *or* wieners (cooked) *or* ham chunks
- 1/4 cup chopped onion
- 8 to 10 medium potatoes, diced
- 1/2 lb. cheese (Velveeta *or* shredded)
- 3 tablespoons flour

Milk

Boil potatoes and onion together until barely soft. Pour off most of water and add milk level with contents. Add sausage and ham base and heat to boiling. Meanwhile add 3 tablespoons of flour

to 1 cup of milk in a shaker. Shake well and add to mixture as soon as it starts to bubble. Add cheese in chunks or shredded. Stir and let set for 5 to 10 minutes. Serves approximately 4 to 6.
　　—Linda Weaver, Middlefield OH

◆ KITCHEN CHAT ◆

BREAKFAST was on the table when Mark came in from milking. We had eggs, sausage, grape nuts, Danish rolls and grape juice from our own grapes.

Later, Mom came over to help me can some chunky beef soup. Mark loves this soup in his thermos during cold winter days when he's working outside.

Dad came over for lunch as Mom was helping me get vegetables ready for the soup. We had noodles, sausage, baked beans, cheese, apple sauce, ice cream and some of Mom's apple pie.

After tucking the children in their beds for an afternoon nap, I finished putting the soup together and started cold-packing it.
　　—Linda Weaver, Dundee, Ohio

Chunky Beef Soup

- 2-1/2 gal. water
- 4 large cans beef broth
- 8 qts. tomato juice
- 4 cups brown sugar
- 4 large onions, cut up fine
- 2 cans beef soup mix
- 1/2 cup salt
- 1 stick butter
- 8 qts. carrots, diced
- 6 qts. peas
- 8 qts. potatoes, diced
- 4 qts. green beans
- 20 lbs. hamburger

Mushrooms

- 4 qts. roast beef cut fine

Salt and cook carrots, peas, potatoes and green beans. Heat all other ingredients (except hamburger, roast beef and mushrooms) to boiling and add vegetables. Fry hamburger with mushrooms and salt and pepper. Add drippings from hamburger to soup. Add roast beef and its drippings. Make thick with clear gelatin. Makes 60 quarts.
　　—Linda Weaver, Dundee OH

Walter Troyer

Breads and Spreads

Pancakes

- 1-1/4 cups flour
- 3 tablespoons sugar
- 3 teaspoons baking powder
- 3/4 teaspoon salt
- 1 egg
- 3 tablespoons butter melted
- 1 cup milk

Mix ingredients together and add butter. Feel free to add more milk to please your texture.
—*Nina Bontrager, Hicksville, Ohio*

Mount Mary's College Doughnuts

- 1 cup shortening
- 1 cup sugar
- 1 cup mashed potatoes
- 2 tablespoons salt
- 1 qt. milk, scalded
- 2 tablespoons dry yeast (2 pkgs.)
- 2 teaspoons nutmeg
- 2 tablespoons vanilla
- 6 egg yolks
- 11 cups flour (half of this could be whole wheat)

Glaze

- 2 lbs. powdered sugar
- 14 tablespoons water

Cool milk and add yeast. Let dissolve. Mix together shortening, sugar, potatoes, salt, milk and yeast. Add nutmeg, vanilla, egg yolks and flour. Don't let dough get too stiff. Let rise one hour. Roll out and cut. Let rise 1-1/2 to 2 hours and fry in deep fat that's been preheated to almost smoking stage. Makes 45 to 60 doughnuts depending on size.
—*Elizabeth Byler, Lobelville TN*

Hot Pepper Butter

- 42 hot peppers
- 1 pt. yellow mustard
- 1 qt. vinegar
- 6 cups sugar
- 1 tablespoon salt
- 1 cup flour
- 1-1/2 cups water

Grind peppers. Add mustard, vinegar, sugar and salt and bring to a boil. Make a paste with flour and water and add to boiling mixture and cook 5 minutes. Makes 7 quarts.
—*Ella Detweiler, Atlantic PA*

◆ KITCHEN CHAT ◆

I GOT UP at 5:30 and wrote some letters. Breakfast was fried potatoes, an egg and bread with my homemade apple butter.

At 8:00 I went next door to Dad's house and fixed breakfast for him and Mom, and afterward washed all the dishes together. Then I got ready to make a batch of apple butter.

By 10:00 I had 3 gallons of apples cored and quartered and in the big stainless steel canner. I added sugar, cinnamon and vinegar and got it on the fire.

Lunch was leftover chicken and potatoes. Later, Dad and his cousin went to the auction with 30 of brother Ben's watermelons. They didn't go for much—some only 75¢.

I quilted until the apple butter was ready and then canned it and got 19 pints. When the jars were cool, I put labels on them and they were ready to sell.
—*Susan Byler, Spartansburg, Pennsylvania*

Drusilla's Special Zucchini Bread

- 3 eggs
- 2 cups sugar
- 1 cup vegetable oil
- 1 teaspoon vanilla
- 1 teaspoon cinnamon
- 1 teaspoon salt
- 1 teaspoon baking soda
- 1/4 teaspoon baking powder
- 3 cups flour (half whole wheat)
- 1/2 cup raisins
- 1/2 cup nuts
- 2 cups zucchini (yellow winter squash can be substituted)

In a bowl, mix together eggs, sugar, vegetable oil, vanilla, cinnamon, salt, baking soda, baking powder and flour. Add zucchini, raisins and nuts. Mix well and bake for 1 hour at 350°.
—*Drusilla Hochstetler, West Union OH*

Large photo: Sherry Pardee; inset: Ronald N. Wilson

Apple Butter

      7 lbs. apples (16 cups sauce)
      3 lbs. brown *or* white sugar
      1 cup vinegar *or* cider
      2 tablespoons cinnamon
      1 cup crushed pineapple

Cook apples; put through a strainer. Add remaining ingredients and put in oven. Bake for 3 hours at 350°. Stir occasionally. Makes 5 quarts.

—*Ella Detweiler, Atlantic PA*

Cinnamon Rolls

      2 cups milk, scalded
      1 cup shortening
      1 cup sugar
      1 teaspoon salt
      1 cup mashed potatoes
      2 tablespoons yeast (2 pkgs.)
    1/2 cup warm water
      2 eggs, well beaten
  7-1/2 cups flour

Mix shortening, sugar, salt and mashed potatoes. Pour hot milk over it. Mix and cool to lukewarm. Dissolve yeast in warm water and set 10 minutes and add to first mixture. Add eggs and flour and knead until smooth. Let rise in a greased bowl until double. Punch down and let rise. Knead again. Roll into a rectangle. Spread with butter or oleo. Sprinkle with brown sugar and cinnamon. Roll to desired size. Slice and place on cookie sheets. Let rise until double. Bake at 350° until lightly brown. Cover with caramel icing while warm.

—*Mrs. Eli Miller, Haven KS*

Cherry Coffee Cake

      1 cup margarine
  1-1/2 cups sugar
      4 eggs
      1 teaspoon vanilla

3 cups flour
1-1/2 teaspoons baking powder
1/2 teaspoon salt
1 can cherry pie filling

Glaze

1-1/2 cups powdered sugar
1 tablespoon butter, melted
1/2 teaspoon vanilla
Milk to make a thin glaze

Cream margarine and sugar together. Add eggs one at a time. Beat well after each. Add vanilla. Sift together flour, baking powder and salt. Add to above mixture. Spread 2/3 of dough in a greased 10-1/2 x 15-1/2 jelly roll pan. Cover with pie filling and spoon rest of batter on top. Bake at 350° for 30 to 40 minutes. Drizzle with glaze while warm.
—*Clara Miller, Sugar Creek OH*

Crunch Johnny Cake

3/4 cup white sugar
1 egg, beaten
1 teaspoon baking powder
1 teaspoon baking soda
1/2 cup flour
3/4 teaspoon salt
1 cup sour cream*
1-1/2 cups corn meal

*If you don't have sour cream, you can use 1/4 cup shortening and 1 cup sour milk. Stir together egg and sour cream. Mix in dry ingredients. Bake at 350° for 30 minutes or until golden brown on top. Serve with maple syrup and milk.
—*Leah Kuepfer, Linwood ON*

Carrot Marmalade

1 lb. carrots
1-1/2 lbs. sugar
2 lemons

Clean carrots and cook until done. Mash and add sugar, lemon juice and grated rind of one lemon. Cook 20 minutes, stirring frequently.
—*Lillie Fussner, Stockport OH*

Zucchini Bread

3 cups flour
1-1/2 cups white sugar
1 teaspoon cinnamon
1 teaspoon salt
1 teaspoon baking powder
1 teaspoon baking soda
2 cups shredded zucchini
1 cup chopped nuts
3 eggs beaten
1 cup vegetable oil
1 cup raisins

In a large bowl, stir together dry ingredients plus zucchini, nuts and raisins. Mix eggs and oil; pour over first mixture and stir until well moistened. Put in bread pans or bundt cake pan. Bake at 350°. Mix powdered sugar and water to make a glaze and drizzle over top.—*Mary Miller, Fredericksburg OH*

Coffee Cake

      1-1/2 cups white sugar
      1/2 cup shortening
        2 eggs
        1 cup milk
        3 cups flour
        3 teaspoons baking powder
        1 teaspoon salt

Topping

        1 cup brown sugar
        4 tablespoons flour
        4 teaspoons cinnamon
        4 tablespoons oleo, melted

Glaze

Powdered sugar
Water

Beat sugar, shortening, eggs until light. Add flour, baking powder, salt and shortening mixture alternately with milk. Spread in a 9 x 13 loaf pan and sprinkle with topping. Make a thin glaze and add when cake is cool.   —*Clara Troyer, Clymer NY*

Cottage Cheese Fritters

        2 cups cottage cheese
        2 eggs
      1/2 cup milk
        2 cups flour
        4 teaspoons baking powder
        1 teaspoon salt

Mix like biscuit dough and drop by rounded teaspoons into deep-fry oil. Drain on paper towels. Eat with pancake syrup.   —*Mary Schlabach*
Millersburg OH

◆ KITCHEN CHAT ◆

SINCE the boys leave early for their job at the sawmill, we eat breakfast in two shifts.

After the second shift is eaten, the schoolchildren, Roman and Nancy, do the dishes while I pack lunches for them and Henry Sr. and Jr. who will drive the buggy 7 miles to cut wood on a friend's farm. We don't have a woods on this place, so we always have to go elsewhere for our winter supply of firewood.

It's a nice, sunny day, and I should do my usual Monday chore, the wash. But I decide to work at finishing up my canning instead. I make hot pepper butter and apple butter, using the oven method for the latter, a recipe I got from my mother-in-law.

—Ella Detweiler, Atlantic, Pennsylvania

Pluckets (Yeast Roll Cake)

        1 pkg. yeast
      1/3 cup sugar
      1/4 cup warm water
      1/3 cup oleo, melted
        1 cup milk, scalded
      1/2 teaspoon salt
        3 eggs, beaten
        4 cups flour

Coating

Oleo, melted
        1 cup sugar
        3 tablespoons cinnamon
      1/2 cup nuts

Add sugar, oleo and salt to milk. Dissolve yeast in warm water. When milk is lukewarm, add yeast,

Both photos: Bill Hentosh

eggs and flour. Beat thoroughly. Cover and let rise until double. Take 1 teaspoon of dough and dip into melted oleo, next into coating mixture. Pile loosely in ungreased angle food cake pan. Let rise 30 minutes. Bake at 350° for about 35 to 40 minutes or until done. Turn pan upside down immediately. After it's baked, you just pluck 'em out.

—Susie Schwartz, Seymour MO

❖❖❖

Buttermilk Biscuits

    2 cups flour
1/2 teaspoon salt
    3 teaspoons baking powder
1/2 teaspoon baking soda
    3 tablespoons lard
    1 cup buttermilk

Sift dry ingredients together. Cut in lard until mixture resembles coarse crumbs. Add buttermilk all at once. Mix with fork until it forms a large ball. Turn out on floured board and knead 1/2 minute. Roll out to 3/8 inch thick. Cut with biscuit cutter. Place biscuits on ungreased cookie sheet and bake at 425° for 15 minutes. Makes approximately 2 dozen.

Sausage Gravy

    1 lb. sausage
    4 tablespoons flour
    1 qt. milk
Salt and pepper

Brown sausage in an iron skillet. Pour off grease. Add the flour and brown lightly. Add milk and stir until smooth. Bring to a boil and add more milk until the desired consistency or thickness. Add salt and pepper to taste.
—Lydia Stutzman
Clare MI

Sherry Pardee

Banana Bread

> 3 bananas, mashed
> 1/2 cup butter *or* oleo
> 1 cup sugar
> 2 cups flour
> 1/4 cup nuts *or* 1/2 cup raisins
> 1 teaspoon baking soda

Pinch of salt

Mix and bake in slow oven. Serve with cold milk.

—*Lovina Wengerd, Polk OH*

Yum Yum Coffee Cake

> 1/2 cup butter
> 1 cup sour cream
> 1 cup sugar
> 2 eggs
> 1 teaspoon baking powder
> 1/2 teaspoon salt
> 2 cups flour
> 1 teaspoon baking soda
> 1 teaspoon vanilla

Nut Filling

> 1/2 cup brown sugar
> 1 cup pecans chopped
> 1/2 cup white sugar
> 1 teaspoon cinnamon

Icing

> 1 cup powdered sugar

Milk (enough to make a thin paste)

Cream butter and sugar. Add eggs one at a time. Beat well. Sift dry ingredients together and add alternately with sour cream. Add vanilla. Pour 1/2 of batter in greased 9 x 13 pan. Add 1/2 of nut filling. Pour remaining batter on top and add re-

maining nut filling. Bake at 350° for 40 minutes. Drizzle with thin powdered sugar icing while cake is still hot. —*Sylvia Miller, Coalgate OK*

Coffee Bread

> 2 cups milk, scalded (cooled to lukewarm)
> 1 tablespoon sugar
> 1 pkg. yeast
> 5 to 5-1/2 cups flour, *divided*
> 1/4 cup butter, melted
> 3/4 cup brown sugar
> 2 eggs
> 1 cup raisins
> 1/2 teaspoon salt

Mix together milk, tablespoon of sugar and yeast. Add 3-1/2 cups flour until soft and doughy and let rise until double in size. Add remaining ingredients except 1-1/2 to 2 cups of flour. Blend in flour to make a stiff batter. Place in a 9 x 13 buttered pan. Dust with sugar and cinnamon. Rise again until double. Bake 20 to 30 minutes at 350°.

—*Linda Weaver, Middlefield OH*

Breakfast Rolls

      2 tablespoons yeast
      1 cup warm water
      3 tablespoons sugar
  1-1/8 cups oleo
      2 cups milk scalded
      2 cups mashed potatoes
      2 teaspoons salt
      4 eggs, beaten
      1 cup sugar
     10 cups flour
Brown sugar
Cinnamon

Soften yeast in warm water, adding sugar. Melt oleo in hot milk. After this has cooled to lukewarm, add the rest of the ingredients except brown sugar and cinnamon. Mix until you have a soft dough. Let rise. Roll out in rectangle shape. Brush with melted oleo. Sprinkle with brown sugar and cinnamon. Roll up jelly roll fashion. Slice. Place on greased pan. Let rise until double in size. Bake at 350° for 30 minutes or until golden brown. Frost with caramel frosting.
—*Verna Troyer*
Holmesville OH

Cream Sticks

      2 tablespoons dry yeast (2 pkgs.)
      1 cup warm water
      1 cup milk, scalded
    1/2 cup oleo
    1/2 teaspoon salt

      2 tablespoons sugar
      2 eggs beaten
  5-1/2 cups flour

Mix the yeast and water. Pour milk over the sugar, salt and oleo. When the milk mixture is cooled to lukewarm, add the yeast and water. Add eggs to above mixture. Blend in flour. If still too sticky, add more flour. Let dough rise until double in size. Knead and form into sticks. Let rise again. Deep fry in fat. Make a slit in one side and fill.

Filling

      3 tablespoons flour
      1 cup milk
      1 cup sugar
      1 cup shortening
      1 teaspoon vanilla
  2-1/2 cups powdered sugar

Combine flour and milk and cook. Cream together sugar and shortening. Add flour mixture and vanilla and cream well. Stir in powdered sugar.

Frosting

      1 cup brown sugar
      8 tablespoons oleo
      4 tablespoons milk *or* cream
Powdered sugar
Vanilla

Mix brown sugar, oleo and milk and boil a few minutes. Add powdered sugar and vanilla.
—*Katie Schlabach, Loganville WI*

Bill Hentosh

Whole Wheat Bread

- 3/4 cup brown sugar
- 3/4 cup flour
- 1 tablespoon salt
- 3 cups warm water
- 2 pkgs. dry yeast
- 1-1/2 tablespoons honey
- 3/4 cup vegetable oil
- 1 to 2 cups whole wheat flour
- 6 to 7 cups white flour

Mix together brown sugar, 3/4 cup flour and salt. Add water and stir well. Mix in yeast and let set until it begins to rise. Add honey and vegetable oil and mix thoroughly; finally add flour. Work real well. Put in warm place to rise until double. Work down. Let rise again for about 25 to 30 minutes. Work out in greased bread pans. Let rise until double in size and bake at 325° for 20 to 25 minutes. Makes 4 loaves.
—*Katie Weaver, Dundee OH*

◆ KITCHEN CHAT ◆

WHEN I came in from feeding the animals, my wife, Susie, had our breakfast of fried 'taters, fried eggs and coffee soup ready. Coffee soup is made from hot coffee with sugar, milk and crumbled toasted bread or crackers.

After breakfast I helped with laundry, then Susie helped me dig three rows of potatoes. We also pulled the tomato plants, which were done bearing, and put away the tomato stakes for the winter. We still have a few sweet peppers left and some green beans that don't want to quit blooming.

Later I filled seven empty feed sacks with black walnuts picked up in our front and back yard. There are about that many more left to gather another day. A local market is paying $10 per hundred pounds this year—the highest ever.

Supper was homemade pizza and fresh cooked carrots.

—*Mahlon Schwartz, Seymour, Missouri*

Barbara's Delicious Rolls

- 2 cups milk
- 2 tablespoons sugar
- 2 sticks oleo
- 4-1/2 teaspoons salt
- 2 cups warm water
- 1 cup sugar
- 5 pkgs. yeast
- 6 eggs, beaten
- 12 cups flour

Brown sugar
Cinnamon
Melted butter

Heat together milk, 2 tablespoons sugar, oleo and salt just until the oleo melts. In a bowl, mix water, sugar and yeast. Mix above mixtures together adding eggs. Finally add flour and let rise to double in size. Roll out on floured surface. Spread melted butter over dough and sprinkle with brown sugar and cinnamon. Roll up and cut into slices. Put in pans and let raise to double. Bake. Cool and frost.
—*Barbara Wagler, Grabill IN*

Coffee Cake

Use the same recipe below but omit the pineapple and nuts.

- 4 cups brown sugar
- 1-1/3 cups butter
- 1 cup molasses *or* waffle syrup

Nuts

Combine the above and heat until butter and sugar are melted. Spread in greased pans, sprinkle with nuts. Put slices of rolled dough on top. Bake. When done, turn upside down on another tray or pan. Could also be used with raisins instead of pineapple and nuts or just with sugar and cinnamon.
—*Katie Yoder, Chouteau OK*

Cinnamon Rolls

- 2 cups milk, scalded
- 1-1/2 cups sugar
- 1 cup butter
- 3 teaspoons salt
- 4 pkgs. yeast
- 2 cups warm water
- 4 eggs
- 13 cups flour, *divided*
- 1/4 cup sugar

Cinnamon
Crushed pineapple drained
Nuts

Combine in a bowl the milk, sugar, butter and salt and let cool. Dissolve yeast in warm water. Add eggs and 4 cups flour to milk mixture; beat until smooth. Add yeast. Gradually add 9 cups of flour to make a soft dough. Let rise until double. Punch down and let rise again. Roll out dough in a rectangle. Brush with butter, sprinkle with sugar, cinnamon, pineapple and nuts. Roll like a jelly roll and slice. Bake at 350° for 25 minutes or until golden brown.   —Katie Yoder, Chouteau OK

Syrup for Church Peanut Butter

   2 cups packed brown sugar
   1 cup boiling water
   2 tablespoons clear Karo
   1 tablespoon maple flavoring
   1 quart marshmallow cream
Peanut Butter

Bring sugar, water and Karo to a boil. Add maple flavoring. Cool slightly. Mix with peanut butter and marshmallow cream. Triple this recipe for 5 pounds of peanut butter. Spread on bread.
          —Edna Miller, Millersburg IN

Whole Wheat Pancakes

1-1/2 cups whole wheat flour
   1/2 tablespoon baking powder
   3/4 teaspoon salt
     2 eggs, beaten
     1 teaspoon baking soda
     3 tablespoons brown sugar
1-1/2 cups buttermilk *or* sour milk
     3 tablespoons shortening, melted

Mix dry ingredients. Combine eggs, milk and shortening. Add dry ingredients and mix until smooth. Fry on a hot, lightly greased griddle.

Syrup for Pancakes

   1 tablespoon flour
   2 cups white sugar
   2 cups milk
   1 tablespoon butter

Mix flour and sugar together. Add milk. Stir and bring to a boil quickly. Remove from heat immediately; stir in butter. Cream may be used for part of the milk and butter omitted.   —Fannie Yoder, Centerville MI

Jonas Coblentz

Main Dishes

Lawry's Chicken

    1/2 cup vinegar
    1 stick butter (melted)

Take skin off chicken pieces, place in baking pan with butter and vinegar. Sprinkle with Lawry's Seasoned Salt. Bake at 350° for 1-1/2 hours.
—*Ruby Beachy, Sugarcreek, Ohio*

Chicken Cordon Bleu

    6 skinless chicken breasts
      (cut up bite-size)
    2 cups cracker crumbs
    4 eggs, beaten
    1/4 lb. ham, cubed
    1/4 lb. sliced Swiss cheese

Dip chicken pieces in eggs, then roll in cracker crumbs. Brown in shortening. Put in oblong pan. Top with ham and cheese.

Sauce

Mix and add:

    1/2 cup sour cream
    1 can cream of chicken soup

Heat 5 minutes. Pour over top and bake at 375° for 30 to 45 minutes.
—*Ruby Beachy*
Sugarcreek OH

Mmmpossible Chicken Broccoli Pie

    3 cups shredded cheddar cheese
    1-1/2 cups cooked and cut up chicken
    1/2 cup finely chopped onion
    1 10 oz. pkg. frozen chopped
      broccoli, thawed and drained
    1-1/2 cups milk
    3 eggs
    3/4 cup Bisquick baking mix
    1/4 teaspoon pepper
    1/2 teaspoon dried thyme leaves

Mix 2 cups of the cheddar, the chicken, onion and broccoli in greased 10 x 1-1/2 pie plate. Beat remaining ingredients except cheese with wire whisk or hand beater until almost smooth, about 1 minute; pour into plate. Bake until knife inserted in center comes out clean, 25 to 35 minutes. Top with remaining cheese. Bake just until melted, 1 to 2 minutes. Cool 5 minutes. Serves 6 to 8.
—*Louella Borntrager, Sugarcreek OH*

Poor Man's Steak

    2 lbs. hamburger
    1 cup milk
    1/2 cup chopped onion
    1/2 teaspoon Worcestershire sauce
Salt and pepper

(I like 1-1/2 teaspoons Worcestershire sauce.) Mix well, press in cookie sheet. Chill overnight. Cut in squares. Brown on each side; put in roaster; pour cream of mushroom soup over top. Bake 45 minutes to 1 hour.
—*Ida Borntregar, Lavalle WI*

◆ *KITCHEN CHAT* ◆

I WAS alone this evening and had just a sandwich for supper. My thoughts went back to when all 11 children were still at home, plus my mother and brother, and there were 15 of us at the table.

I cooked in big kettles each meal and often made many skillets of fried mush for breakfast and 15 eggs, as everyone had good appetites.

It seemed the food tasted much better cooked in large amounts. Now sometimes I get lonesome for those days when we were one big, happy family.
—Mrs. LaVern Steury, Quincy, Michigan

Juicy Meat Loaf

    2 lbs. ground beef
    2 eggs, well beaten
    3/4 cup tomato juice
    3/4 cup quick oats uncooked
    1/4 cup chopped onion
    2 teaspoons salt
    1/4 teaspoon pepper

Combine all ingredients thoroughly. Pack firmly in loaf pan. Bake at 350° for 1 hour. If a sauce is desired, mix 2 tablespoons each of ketchup, mustard and brown sugar and spread over meat loaf before baking.
—*Erma Beechy, Millersburg OH*

Ronald N. Wilson

Mock Steak

3 lbs. ground beef
2 cups bread crumbs
1 can cream of mushroom soup
1 cup water
1 teaspoon each salt, pepper

Mix meat, water, bread crumbs, salt and pepper. Press into cookie sheet and let stand in refrigerator overnight. Cut in squares. Roll in flour and brown; add soup and water. Simmer for 1 hour. Soup will thicken for gravy.　　—Susan D. Byler
Spartansburg PA

Chicken Dressing 'n' Stuff

6 cups bread crumbs, browned
1/4 cup chopped celery
1 teaspoon parsley flakes
1 teaspoon chopped onion
2 eggs
1/4 cup butter
Salt and pepper to taste

Mix all ingredients and add enough hot water to moisten. Place in greased casserole.

Topping

1/4 cup butter
1 cup chicken broth
1 cup cream of chicken soup
1 cup cream of celery soup
Salt and pepper

Melt butter and thicken with flour; add broth, salt and pepper. Cook until thick. Add the soups. Pour over dressing. Bake at 350° for 45 minutes.
—Susan D. Byler, Spartansburg PA

Amish Dressing

3 large carrots, diced (cook till soft)
2 large potatoes, diced
1 cup diced celery
1/2 cup diced onion
1/2 teaspoon sage
1 teaspoon salt
1/2 teaspoon pepper
1 cup diced chicken and broth
1 loaf bread, cubed and toasted

Mix together and add to above:

2 tablespoons flour
2 cup milk
1 egg

Bake 1 hour at 350°.
—Edna Bontrager, La Grange IN

Meat Loaf Topped With Mashed Potatoes

2 lbs. ground beef
1 cup cracker crumbs
1 medium onion, diced
3 eggs
Salt and pepper
1/2 cup catsup

Mix together in loaf. Put catsup on top and bake till done. Put mashed potatoes on top of meat loaf. Top with Velveeta cheese and warm up.
—Edna Bontrager, La Grange IN

◆ KITCHEN CHAT ◆

BREAKFAST was fried mashed potatoes and warmed-up Salisbury steak, left over from a Saturday evening dinner. We serve dinner groups by reservation. We had 15 guests on Saturday and will have a group of 60 next week.

Last night we had a hard frost, so this morning I started cleaning out our large garden and bringing in the last of the produce. First were the sweet potatoes—had a short row with at least 3 bushels. The largest one was 12 inches long and weighed in at 4 pounds, 9 ounces.

Next I gathered a 5-quart pail of ground cherries. My wife, Mattie, makes these into pies and takes those and other baked goods to the Farmers' Market in South Bend.

—Eldon Rapp, Bremen, Indiana

Chipped Beef Potpie

    1 cup chopped onion
  1/4 cup hot fat
  1/4 teaspoon pepper and salt
    2 cups peas
  1/4 oz. dried beef, cut up*
    2 tablespoons flour
    2 cups carrots
    2 cups water
    2 cups sliced potatoes
    1 bouillon cube

Pastry

  1-1/2 cups flour
    1/2 teaspoon paprika
    1/4 teaspoon pepper
      3 tablespoons baking powder
    1/2 teaspoon celery salt
      5 tablespoons lard
    3/4 cup milk
      1 teaspoon salt

Pastry: Mix dry ingredients; add lard and mix like pie dough. Stir in milk. Drop on potpie and bake for 25 to 30 minutes at 345°. To make potpie: Saute onions and beef in hot fat. Stir in flour and seasonings. Add remaining ingredients and bring to a boil. Cover and simmer till soft. Pour hot mixture into casserole and drop dough on top; bake.
*Chicken, stew meat or pork may be used instead of dried beef.　　　—Cora Byler, Middlefield OH

◆ KITCHEN CHAT ◆

DINNER today was a common meal of mashed potatoes, poor man's steak and gravy and tossed salad. Dessert was home-canned fruit and apple bars.

We run a bulk food store, and our hours are whenever we have light in the shop. So, between other chores, I waited on customers. In the afternoon I weighed out 30 bags of angel food cake mix, 20 bags for one order. We buy flours and sugars in 100-pound bags and weigh it out into smaller bags, which makes a lot of scooping.

After school the neighbor children came in and helped me move dishes and groceries from our summer kitchen in the basement to the upstairs kitchen. Their help was appreciated!
　　　—Edna Schlabach, Winesburg, Ohio

Taco El Plato

Meat Sauce

- 1 lb. ground beef
- 1 envelope French's Taco Seasoning Mix
- 2 cups water
- 3/4 cup pre-cooked rice

Salad

- 1 small head lettuce, shredded (about 4 cups)
- 2 to 3 tomatoes, diced
- 1/4 cup prepared French dressing

Toppings

Chopped onion
Shredded cheddar cheese
Prepared bottled taco sauce, if desired

Brown beef in skillet, stirring to crumble; pour off excess fat. Stir in contents of seasoning mix envelope, water and rice. Bring to a boil, reduce heat and simmer 10 to 15 minutes, stirring occasionally. Combine lettuce, tomatoes and dressing; toss lightly. Serve salad mixture on plates and top with hot meat sauce. Pass onion, cheese and taco sauce to add as desired. Serves 6.

—*Neoma Coblentz, Sweet Springs MO*

◆ KITCHEN CHAT ◆

THIS EVENING three families gathered at the Earls' to process meat from two hogs butchered this morning. Son Jason decided to take along the two deer that he'd shot on Friday, the first day of bow season.

He was pretty pleased to get a nice 8-pt. buck at 8:00 in the morning, and then a doe in the evening. We were thankful for the meat!

The Millers were there, so with the Earls, Ernests and us, we had the first four families that lived in this settlement. Our two teachers, Harley and Chester Miller, also joined us.

The kitchen was a bustle of activity, with some singing being done while working. Soon the meat was in steaks, sausage, deerburgers, etc. We then served fresh cider, cake, ice cream and popcorn mixed with potato chips. We also had some sausage samples.

By the time we had all our meat, grinder, etc., loaded on the big wagon, there was barely room for John and I and the five youngest.

—*Fannie Miller, Sears, Michigan*

Poor Man's Steak

- 1 lb. hamburger
- 1 cup milk
- 1 cup cracker crumbs
- 1/4 teaspoon pepper
- 1 teaspoon salt
- 1 small onion, chopped

Mix all the ingredients well, then shape in narrow loaf. Let it set for at least 8 hours or overnight. Then cut in slices and fry in skillet on both sides until brown. Then put the slices in roaster and spread mushroom soup on each piece. Use 1 can soup. Bake this 1 hour at 325°. Pan gravy may be used with the mushroom soup if desired.

—*Ella Hershberger, Oakland MO*

Doyle Yoder

Omelette Souffle

- 12 eggs, well beaten
- 1 teaspoon salt
- 1 teaspoon dry mustard
- 3 cups milk
- 1-1/2 lbs. sausage *or* ham cut bite-size (sausage should be fried out a little but not browned, then drained)
- 6 slices bread, cubed
- 1 cup shredded cheese

Mix all together. Pour in 9 x 13 pan. Bake at 325° to 350° till set. Take out and cut in blocks and turn over and top with shredded cheese, cheese sauce or Velveeta slices. Put back in oven for another 5 to 10 minutes. Makes 12 nice portions and can be reheated.

—*Mary Hostetler, Danville OH*

Amos Graber

Golden Ham Casserole

  2 cups diced cooked ham
  2 cups cubed potatoes
  1 cup sliced carrots
  2 tablespoons chopped onion
  1 cup diced celery

Sauce

  3 tablespoons butter
  2 tablespoons flour
1-1/2 cups milk
  1/2 cup cheese
Dash of salt and pepper

Brown ham and onions in 3 tablespoons oleo. Cook together potatoes, carrots and celery until almost done. Drain. Heat sauce ingredients together. Put vegetables and meat in casserole dish by layers. Pour sauce over all. Sprinkle with buttered bread or cracker crumbs. Bake at 375° for 30 to 35 minutes. —*Laura Brenneman, Morley MI*

Haystack Supper

  1/2 lb. soda crackers, crushed
    4 lbs. hamburger
    4 cups cooked rice
    2 heads lettuce, cut up
    1 big pkg. corn chips, crushed
    6 tomatoes, diced
    1 cup chopped nuts
    1 onion, chopped
    2 jars pizza sauce
    2 cans cheddar cheese soup
1-1/2 cans milk

Brown hamburger with onions; drain off fat. Add pizza sauce. Heat milk and cheese soup together. Put ingredients on plate in order given; soup goes on last. Serves 14. —*Fannie Yoder*
Millersburg OH

Super Duper Casserole

    1 lb. hamburger
  1/2 cup onions
    2 tablespoons oleo
  1/2 teaspoon pepper
    1 teaspoon salt
    1 pkg. noodles
    1 can mushroom soup
    1 can cream of chicken soup
    1 can tomato soup
Potato chips

Cook noodles, drain. Brown hamburger and onions. Mix all ingredients. Bake at 350° for 1/2 hour. Delicious.
—*Clara Coblentz, Jackson Center PA*

Ronald N. Wilson

Turkey or Chicken Supreme

        2 cups cooked and diced chicken
        2 cups uncooked macaroni
        2 cups milk
        2 cans cream of chicken soup
        1 medium onion
      1/2 teaspoon salt
      1/4 teaspoon pepper
        3 tablespoons melted oleo

Combine and pour these ingredients in greased casserole. Refrigerate overnight. Remove from refrigerator several hours before baking. Bake at 350°, for 1-1/2 hours. Top with Velveeta cheese spread during last part of baking.

—Katie Erb, Dundee OH

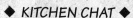

> ◆ **KITCHEN CHAT** ◆
>
> THE SMELL of lunch and the warmth of the Friendly Maid cookstove were so welcome after being outside all forenoon.
>
> Neighbor Jerry Miller gave me and each of the other widows in our community a turkey yesterday. Daughter Hannah and I had the wings wrapped in foil and baking all forenoon. We enjoyed them with fried potatoes and rounded things out with applesauce and canned sweet cherries.
>
> We'll can the rest of the turkey tomorrow, as it weighs 15 pounds and is too much for us to eat all at once.
>
> —Polly Anna Stoll, Aylmer, Ontario

Tomato Gravy

        1 quart tomato juice
        2 teaspoons salt
Dash of red pepper
        2 quarts milk
    1-1/2 cups flour

Bring tomato juice to a boil. Add salt and pepper. Pour in the milk all at once and heat. Take the flour and mix with enough milk to make gravy. Do not let the juice and milk boil before adding gravy as it may curdle. When juice and milk are hot but not boiling, add gravy and stir constantly till boils. Serve over fried potatoes, cornmush, pancakes, omelets, biscuits or just eggs and bread.

—Lizzie Kauffman, Holton MI

Enchiladas

        3 lbs. hamburger
        1 can tomato paste, 6 oz.
        2 lbs. colby cheese, grated
      12 flour tortillas
        2 batches enchilada sauce

Brown hamburger and drain off fat. Add tomato paste and one batch of enchilada sauce, mix well. Put approximately 3/4 cup of meat mixture in middle of flour tortilla and about 1/4 cup cheese and roll tortilla up and place seam side down on greased baking dish, side by side. Make another batch of sauce using only 1/2 of spices. (I let this simmer while rolling the tortillas up.) Spread this over top and cover with rest of the cheese. Bake at 350° for 1/2 hour. Serve topped with lettuce, sour cream and salsa.

Enchilada Sauce

        1 can (15 oz.) tomato sauce
      1/2 cup water
    2-1/2 teaspoons chili powder
      1/2 teaspoon salt
      1/2 teaspoon garlic powder
      1/4 teaspoon ground cumin
        5 to 6 drops tabasco

Combine all and simmer 20 minutes.

—Ruth Raber, Millersburg OH

Homemade Pizza

Dough

        1 cup warm water
        4 tablespoons shortening
        1 pkg. dry yeast
      1/4 teaspoon salt
        4 cups sifted flour

Roll out and line bottom of two oblong cake pans.

Topping

        1 small onion
        2 tablespoons salad oil
        1 pint tomato juice
        1 bay leaf
        1 teaspoon salt
        1 tablespoon sugar
      1/2 teaspoon oregano
Dash pepper
        1 pt. hamburger

Grate cheese over top and bake.

—Verda Petersheim, Six Lakes MI

Poor Man's Steak

1-1/2 lbs. hamburger
1/2 cup cracker crumbs
1/2 cup cold water
Salt and pepper to taste

Mix well and form into a loaf. Put in refrigerator overnight. Cut in slices, roll in flour and fry in butter. Put in casserole or roaster and cover with one can of cream of mushroom soup. Dilute the soup with one can water. Bake 1-1/2 hours at 300°.

—*Mary Schlabach, Apple Creek OH*

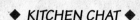

```
◆ KITCHEN CHAT ◆
```

WE GOT UP at 5:00, and the boys did our few chores. We milk only one Jersey cow to keep the family supplied with milk, cream and homemade butter. We also have hens for eggs and meat-type chickens, plus six big turkeys.

Breakfast consisted of baked eggs with homemade bread, corn flakes, cookies and tea. Afterward, the girls did dishes and helped Mom pack school lunches while the boys put water in our big kettle and put the fire under it to heat for washing.

—*Joe Slabaugh, Viroqua, Wisconsin*

Shipwreck Stew

1-1/2 lbs. hamburger
Onions sliced *or* dried
1 quart potatoes, cooked and diced
1 pint carrots, cooked and diced
8 oz. noodles, cooked
1 pint peas
1 can cream of chicken soup
1 can cream of celery soup
1 can mushroom soup

Place in order in casserole and bake at 350° for 1 hour. Put Velveeta slices on top of casserole.

—*Mary Troyer, Applecreek OH*

Overnight Casserole

1 cup uncooked macaroni
1 can cream of mushroom soup
3 tablespoons butter
1/2 cup diced onion
1 cup chopped ham
1-1/2 cup milk
1 cup diced Velveeta cheese

Mix together and put in refrigerator. Stir a couple times. Can also be stirred together in the morning with good results. Bake for 2 hours at 350°. Serves 6.

—*Barbara Troyer, New Wilmington PA*

Ben Coblentz

Sherry Pardee

Chicken Casserole

    9 slices bread
    4 cups cut up cooked chicken
    1 can mushroom pieces
 1/2 cup salad dressing
    4 eggs
    2 cups milk or part chicken broth
    9 slices Velveeta cheese
    2 cans celery soup
 1/4 cup butter

Grease the casserole or roaster with butter. Break bread in bottom of casserole. Put chicken and mushroom pieces on top. Beat eggs, milk and salad dressing and pour on top of bread and chicken. Cover with cheese and put celery soup on top and refrigerate overnight. Bake at 350° for 1-1/2 hours. Stir it a little every so often so the liquid goes down to the bread and is absorbed. This expands when baking, so be sure to use a big enough casserole.

—Mrs. Paul Troyer
Mount Hope OH

Dumplings

    4 eggs, beaten
    1 teaspoon salt
Flour to make stiff dough

During this time I'll put on the stove 1 quart beef juice and a small onion cut up and let it get to boiling while rolling out dough. Cut dough in squares with pizza cutter, and when juice boils, put them in and cook. Stir it. May have to add water, salt and pepper to taste.

—Anna Wickey
Beane IN

Haystack Supper

 1/2 lb. crushed cheese crackers or
      crackers of your choice
    1 7-oz. box quick or regular rice
    6 tomatoes, diced
    1 head lettuce, shredded
    2 sweet onions, diced
    2 lbs. hamburger
    1 quart tomato sauce
    1 lb. corn chips, crushed
1-1/2 cups chopped pecans

White Sauce

    2 cups milk
    3 tablespoons flour
    1 tablespoon butter
Velveeta or cheddar cheese
Salt to taste

Cook rice as directed. Fry hamburger and add to tomato sauce and heat together. Serve in order given on top of each other, which makes your haystack. You can also use 1 can cheddar cheese soup and 1 soup can of milk instead of white sauce.

—Viola Schrock, Arcola IL

Spicy Oven-Fried Chicken

   1/2 **cup yellow cornmeal**
   1/2 **cup all-purpose flour**
 1-1/2 **teaspoons salt**
 1-1/2 **teaspoons chili powder**
   1/2 **teaspoon crushed oregano leaves**
   1/4 **teaspoon pepper**
    2 **to 3-1/2 lbs. broiler-fryer, cut up**
   1/2 **cup milk**
   1/3 **cup butter or margarine, melted**

Combine cornmeal, flour, salt, chili powder, oregano and pepper. Dip chicken pieces in milk; coat with corn meal mixture. Place chicken, skin side up, in large shallow baking pan. Drizzle butter over chicken. Bake in preheated 375° oven about 50 to 55 minutes or until done. Variation substitute 1 teaspoon crushed basil leaves for chili powder.
—*Elizabeth Stutzman, Curtiss WI*

Chicken Gumbo Casserole

   9 **slices bread, cubed**
   4 **cups cooked and diced chicken**
 1/4 **cup butter, melted**
 1/2 **cup mayonnaise**
   4 **eggs, well beaten**
   1 **cup milk**
   1 **cup chicken broth**
   1 **teaspoon salt**

   9 **slices Velveeta cheese**
   2 **cans cream of celery or chicken soup**

Take off crusts of bread and set aside. Mix together butter, milk, mayonnaise, chicken broth, eggs and salt. Add undiluted soup. Place bread in bottom of dish greased with butter; layer chicken over bread. Next, layer soup mixture over chicken. Cover with cheese. Brown bread crusts with 1/4 cup melted butter. Place on top. Bake for 1-1/4 hours at 350° uncovered.
—*Esther Troyer Sugarcreek OH*

◆ KITCHEN CHAT ◆

OUR SUPPER tonight was creamed potatoes, pizza casserole and applesauce. For dessert we had strawberries and oatmeal cookies.

We froze around 90 quarts of strawberries last spring. Needless to say, husband Obed and I were tired of picking. Sometimes our granddaughters helped, but it was easier for them to see airplanes and birds than berries!

After supper dishes were done, I took the dried apples out of our solar fruit drier, which a neighbor made for us. It worked great this summer with our extra-warm days. There are four shelves in it, and we filled it three times this summer. Now we have over 2 gallons of dried apple snitz to use later for pies.
—Verna Troyer, Holmesville, Ohio

Chicken Rice Casserole

   2 cups rice cooked in 2-1/2 cups chicken broth (20 minutes, covered, on low heat)
   2 cups celery sauteed lightly in oleo
   2 cups mushroom soup, undiluted
1-1/2 cups real mayonnaise
   2 tablespoons chopped onion
   2 cups chicken chopped (picked off bone)

Mix gently, put in greased casserole. Put crushed cornflakes mixed with oleo on top. Bake at 350° for 45 minutes.
                —Susie Yoder, Baltic OH

Ham Casserole

   4 cups diced cooked ham
   4 tablespoons margarine
   1 tablespoon Worcestershire sauce
1/2 cup chopped onion

Combine and cook until onions are tender. Place in bottom of roaster.

   2 cans cream of mushroom soup
   1 cup milk
   2 cups cubed yellow cheese

Heat together until cheese is melted. Place over first mixture.

   4 quarts cooked and mashed potatoes
   1 cup sour cream

Mix potatoes and sour cream. Place on top of mixture and sprinkle with crumbled bacon. Bake at 350° for 20 minutes. The soup and cheese mixture comes to the top when done.
             —Emma Weaver, Greenwood NY

Wigglers

   9 slices bacon
   3 lbs. hamburger
   3 onions chopped
   3 cups cut and cooked carrots
   2 cans peas
   1 stalk celery, cut and cooked
   2 lbs. spaghetti, cooked
   3 cups diced potatoes
   2 cans mushroom soup
   1 lb. Velveeta cheese
1-1/2 to 2 quarts tomato soup

Fry bacon; take out. Fry hamburger and onions in bacon grease. Put in large roaster. Add potatoes, carrots, celery, peas, spaghetti and mushroom soup. Then arrange cheese slices and bacon on top. Pour tomato soup over all. Bake in oven 350° to 375° for 1-1/2 to 2 hours.
              —Mary Troyer
              Glasgow KY

Jiffy Pizza

Dough

   2 cups flour
   1 tablespoon baking powder
   1 teaspoon salt
2/3 cup milk
1/3 cup salad oil

Sift flour, baking powder and salt together. Add milk and oil. Press dough in bottom of pan. Spread 1 quart pizza sauce on dough. Crumble 1 pound browned hamburger on top and sprinkle with shredded cheese. Bake 25 to 30 minutes at 425°.

Pizza Sauce

   1 pkg. tomatoes
2/3 teaspoon garlic powder
1-1/2 lbs. onions
   2 hot peppers *or* 1/2 teaspoon red pepper
3/4 tablespoon sweet basil
3/4 tablespoon oregano
3/4 cup sugar
   2 tablespoons salt
   1 cup vegetable oil

Put all ingredients together and simmer until it comes to a full boil. Make a paste of 1 cup flour and water. Add to boiling mixture and bring to boil again. Serves 6 or more.
             —Marie Yoder, Scottville MI

One-Dish Meal

        4 large potatoes, cubed
        1 lb. ground chuck
        1 teaspoon salt
Dash pepper
        1 can kidney beans, drained
        1 small onion, chopped
        1 10-oz. can tomato soup
     1/4 cup water

Peel and cube potatoes. Place 1/2 of potatoes in a greased 2-quart casserole dish. Add ground chuck, salt and pepper, beans and onion. Arrange remaining potatoes on top. Combine soup and water, pour over all. Put cover on dish. Bake 1-1/2 hours in a pre-heated oven 350°. Serves 4 to 6.
        —Josephine Schwartz, Berne IN

Filsa (Casserole)

     1/2 cup celery cooked and chopped
     1/2 cup carrots cooked and chopped
     1/2 cup potatoes cooked and cubed
        1 cup cooked chicken meat chopped
           with broth
     1/2 teaspoon pepper

     1/2 teaspoon sage (optional)
     1/2 teaspoon thyme (optional)
        1 teaspoon salt
        4 eggs
        2 cups milk
        2 cups toasted bread crumbs

Combine all the ingredients in a large bowl. Put in 12 x 9 baking pan. Bake at 350° for 40 to 45 minutes or until golden brown. Very good with chicken gravy. Serves 6 to 8.   —Daniel Hershberger
        Ethridge TN

Calico Beans

Brown:

        1 lb. hamburger
        1 large onion, chopped
        5 strips bacon, cut up

Mix in a casserole:

     1/2 cup ketchup
     3/4 cup brown sugar
        1 tablespoon mustard
        1 tablespoon vinegar

Add:

        1 15-16 oz. baked beans
        1 15-16 oz. kidney beans
        1 15-16 oz. butter beans

Mix all together and bake 1 hour at 325°.
        —Sarah Hershberger, Guys Mills PA

Sour Cream Beef 'n' Noodle Bake

        1 pkg. (8 oz.) egg noodles
        1 lb. ground chuck
     1/2 cup chopped onion
        1 can (8 oz.) tomato sauce
        1 teaspoon salt
     1/8 teaspoon pepper
     1/2 teaspoon garlic salt
        1 cup cottage cheese
        1 cup sour cream
        1 pkg. (8 oz.) cheddar cheese, shredded

Cook noodles; drain. Brown meat and onions together; add tomato sauce, salt, pepper and garlic salt. Combine noodles, cottage cheese and sour cream; put half in bottom of 2-1/2 quart casserole. Add half the meat mixture. Repeat layers. Top with cheese. Bake at 350° for 25 to 30 minutes. Serves 6-8.   —Fannie A. Schwartz, Bryant IN

Doyle Yoder

Pizza Casserole

- 4 oz. pepperoni, sliced thin
- 4 oz. grated swiss cheese *or* hot pepper cheese
- 4 oz. mushrooms, drained
- 2 16 oz. jars pizza sauce
- 8 oz. sausage *or* ground beef, browned
- 8 oz. thin spaghetti, cooked and drained
- 1/2 stick butter *or* oleo
- 1/4 cup diced onion
- 1/4 cup diced red or green pepper
- 1/4 teaspoon salt
- 1/4 teaspoon pepper
- 1/2 teaspoon oregano

Saute onion and pepper in butter or oleo. Drain butter or oleo into bottom of 9 x 13 baking dish. Cover with spaghetti. Spread 1 jar of pizza sauce over spaghetti. Layer pepperoni, sausage, cheese, onions, peppers, mushrooms and spices on top. Cover with second jar of pizza sauce and layer of swiss cheese. Cover with foil, making sure the foil doesn't touch the cheese. Bake at 350° for 45 minutes.　　—*Mrs. Aden Mullet, Fredericksburg OH*

Chicken Patties

- 2 lbs. ground chicken
- 1 egg
- 1/4 teaspoon pepper
- 1/2 cup crushed crackers
- 1/4 cup milk
- 1-1/4 teaspoon salt

Mix all together and make patties. Bake at 350° for 45 minutes or fry in skillet like hamburgers.
—*Clara Weaver, Dundee OH*

> ◆ *KITCHEN CHAT* ◆
> *WE HAD a light lunch of sandwiches and cherry pie and then worked in the garden.*
>
> *There are still a few tomatoes, plus carrots and several delicious watermelons. We had everything in before supper, which was pancakes and sausage.*
>
> —*Josephine Schwartz, Berne, Indiana*

Taco Salad

- 1 head lettuce, chopped
- 1 lb. hamburger
- 8 oz. cheddar cheese
- 1 small can kidney beans
- 1 large onion chopped
- 4 medium tomatoes, diced
- 1 pkg. taco-flavored chips
- 1 pkg. taco seasoning

Dressing

- 8 oz. thousand island dressing
- 1/3 cup sugar
- 1 tablespoon taco sauce
- 1 tablespoon taco seasoning

Brown hamburger. Add taco seasoning; reserve 1 tablespoon for dressing. Select a large salad bowl, allowing enough room to toss at serving time. Layer salad ingredients in bowl, starting with lettuce and ending with cheese. Cover and refrigerate. At serving time, toss salad with dressing and chips.
—Mattie Mast, Wilmot OH

Oven-Baked Chicken

Young broilers *or* fryers
- 1 cup crushed cornflakes
- 1 cup crushed soda crackers
- 2 teaspoons salt
- 1 teaspoon pepper
- 2 tablespoons seasoned salt

Combine ingredients and mix well. Beat 1 egg and add 1 cup milk. Dip chicken pieces into egg/milk mixture, then roll in crumbs and place on buttered cookie sheet and bake in oven 400° for 30 minutes. Turn meat, reduce heat to 375° and bake for 30 minutes more.
—Gertrude Mast
Jamestown PA

Mock Ham Loaf

- 1 lb. hamburger
- 1/2 lb. hot dogs, ground fine
- 1 cup cracker crumbs
- 1 teaspoon salt

Dash of pepper
1 egg

Glaze

3/4 cup brown sugar
1/2 cup water
1/2 teaspoon mustard
1 tablespoon vinegar

Combine all the ingredients. Add 1/2 of glaze recipe to above ingredients. Mix well. Shape in loaf and bake at 350° for 1-1/2 hours. Baste occasionally with glaze. —*Sadie Yoder, Blue River WI*

◆ KITCHEN CHAT ◆

YESTERDAY we joined 20 other families for church services in a neighbor's home, which is what we do instead of having a church house. After services we were served a light lunch of Swiss cheese and ham sandwiches, pickles, coffee and cookies.

Today after the wash was on the line, we had a quick lunch of pork and beans, summer sausage sandwiches, apple crisp and ice cream.

We have plenty of summer sausage and trail bologna since my husband Obed and our sons got ten deer and an elk last season. The older deer are made into bologna and summer sausage by a neighboring family that runs a meat business. Meat from the younger deer is ground and frozen or cut into chunks and canned.

—*Verna Troyer, Holmesville, Ohio*

A Cookout

2-1/2 lbs. hamburger
12 soda crackers, crushed
1 egg
Salt and pepper to taste

Mix all together and form patties. Line a sheet cake pan or cookie sheet with tin foil. Layer a dab of butter, slice of onion and hamburger. Slice carrots and potatoes and put over top of hamburgers. Add salt and pepper to taste. Put another sheet of foil over top, always the shiny side on the inside. Roll top and bottom edges together and fold 3 times all the way around so it is sealed. Bake 1-1/2 hours at 350°. —*Edna Miller*
Fredericksburg OH

My Favorite Pizza Recipe

2 cups Bisquick flour
2 cups all-purpose flour
6 teaspoons baking powder
1/2 teaspoon salt
2/3 cup vegetable oil
1-1/3 cups milk

Mix and spread on a cookie sheet. Bake at 350° for 15 minutes.

Pizza Topping

1 lb. ground sausage *or* hamburger
1/4 cup chopped onion fried in tablespoon of butter
1 cup pizza sauce *or* ketchup

Put on top of crust and top with Velveeta cheese slices. Bake at 350° for 15 minutes.
—*Amanda Yoder, Baltic OH*

Chicken Meat Patties

2 lbs. ground chicken
2 eggs
1 onion (optional)
1 cup cracker crumbs
1 cup milk
1/2 teaspoon salt
1/2 teaspoon seasoned salt (or to taste)

Mix above ingredients well. Make patties. Roll in flour and fry in butter. For variety, use same recipe for chicken meat loaf. Also a deeper pan may be used and mashed potatoes added on top when done. —*Lydiann Miller, Millersburg OH*

Garden Supper Casserole

- 2 cups cubed soft bread
- 1/2 cup cubed cheese
- 2 tablespoons butter, melted
- 1 cup peas
- 1-1/2 cups cream sauce
- 2 tablespoons chopped onion
- 3 hard-cooked eggs, sliced
- 1 large tomato, sliced

Cream Sauce

- 3 tablespoons butter
- 3 tablespoons flour
- 1/4 teaspoon salt
- 1 cup milk

Mix bread cubes, cheese and butter. Spread 1/2 of mixture in greased 1-quart baking dish. Add peas, half of cream sauce. Brown the onions in butter. Add eggs. Pour over peas. Arrange tomatoes over top and cover with remaining cream sauce. Add remaining bread mixture. Bake at 350° for 25 minutes. —Lydiann Miller, Millersburg OH

Mock Turkey and Dressing

- 1 lb. hamburger
- 2 cans cream of chicken soup
- 2 cans cream of mushroom soup
- 1 medium zucchini, thinly sliced *or* shredded
- 2 cans of water
- 5 cups of croutons

Brown hamburger. Add the soup and stir well. Add thinly sliced zucchini. Place croutons in a large casserole. Add other ingredients plus water (more if you like your dressing moist). Bake at 350° for 25 minutes or until brown.

—Katie Miller, Mount Vernon OH

Pizza Casserole

- 1 or 2 lbs. hamburger
- 1/2 green pepper
- 1 can mushroom soup
- 1 pint pizza sauce
- 1 can mushrooms, not drained
- 1/4 teaspoon garlic powder
- 1/4 teaspoon oregano
- 1/4 cup Parmesan cheese
- 8 oz. wide noodles

Mozzarella cheese
Pepperoni

Brown hamburger; add salt, pepper and onion to taste. Cook noodles 3 to 5 minutes. Drain. Place in bottom of baking dish. Add hamburger mixture and remaining ingredients. Top with mozzarella cheese and pepperoni. Bake at 350° for 1/2 hour.

—Maddie Yoder, Millersburg OH

> ### ◆ KITCHEN CHAT ◆
> WE HAD a frost last night, so daughter Miriam went out this morning and picked ground cherries from the bushes that come up "volunteer" every year. I made several ground-cherry pies, which are my husband Tobe's favorite.
>
> For dinner we had chicken, mashed potatoes and gravy, peas, applesauce and pie. Afterward our bread supply was low, so the girls stirred up a batch of dough while I did the dishes.
>
> This afternoon I walked up to the apple orchard and picked up some apples from the ground. The girls made apple dumplings, which we enjoyed tonight with ice cream after chores.
> —Mary Hostetler, Danville, Ohio

Anna K. Wickey

Tostada

- 2 lbs. hamburger, browned
- 1 16 oz. refried beans
- 1 pkg. taco seasoning
- 3/4 cup water

Mix the above, bring to a boil and simmer for 10 minutes. While simmering, prepare the following and put in individual containers:

- 1 pkg. (12-16 oz.) tortilla chips, crushed
- 1 head lettuce, shredded
- 4 tomatoes, chopped
- 1 lb. colby cheese, shredded
- 2 onions, chopped
- 2 qt. cheese sauce, hot
- 16 oz. sour cream
- 16 oz. salsa

When ready to eat, put small amounts of each item on top of each other on your plate in order given: chips, meat, lettuce, tomatoes, cheese, and onions. Top with cheese sauce and garnish with sour cream and salsa. If a microwave is available, the cheese sauce can be eliminated. Put shredded cheese on top and microwave to melt, then garnish.
—Mrs. Daniel J. Miller
Nappanee IN

Chicken 'n' Stuff

- 6 cups bread cubes
- 1/4 cup celery
- 1 tablespoon chopped onion
- 1 tablespoon parsley flakes
- 2 eggs, beaten
- 1/4 cup butter *or* oleo, melted

Salt and pepper

Cream Topping

- 1/4 cup butter *or* oleo
- 4 tablespoons flour
- 1 cup chicken broth

Chicken seasoning

- 1 can cream of chicken soup
- 1 can Pet milk (14 oz.)
- 2 cups cooked chicken

Combine bread cubes, celery, onion, parsley flakes, eggs, butter, salt and pepper. Add enough hot water or broth to moisten. Place in greased casserole. Prepare topping—melt butter, thicken with flour to make paste. Add chicken broth, soup and milk. Cook to a thick gravy. Add chicken; season to taste with chicken seasoning, salt and pepper. Cover and bake at 350° for 40 minutes.
—Fannie Miller, Sherman NY

> ### ◆ KITCHEN CHAT ◆
>
> THIS MORNING finds us in the kitchen ready to tackle the grapes. Daughter Sara Jane washes the jars with the breakfast dishes while I wash the grapes and put them on the stove to cook. Next we put them through a strainer and let them drip awhile while we get another batch ready to cook.
>
> In the middle of doing the jelly, I stir up some coffee bread using an old recipe from Jake's mom. It needs to rise, so I cover it and leave it for a few hours.
>
> Meantime, my friend Nancy Miller comes calling. She tells me to try making grape butter instead of jelly—it takes only half the time. That sounds like a good idea to me, as I've decided making jelly is a big mess!
>
> Daughter Sara Jane fixes us each a salad for lunch, and we decide what cookies to bake this afternoon. She likes to bake oatmeal cookies like my mother used to make, which are a favorite with the men.
>
> —Linda Weaver, Middlefield, Ohio

Chicken Dressing

- 1 20 oz. loaf bread
- 4 medium potatoes, diced
- 1 medium carrot, diced
- 1 celery stalk, diced
- 1/4 cup chicken soup base
- 3 eggs
- 1/4 cup diced onion
- 1/4 teaspoon sage
- 1/4 teaspoon garlic powder
- 1/4 teaspoon black pepper
- 1 pint chicken broth (heat first)
- 2 cups water
- 1/4 cup margarine
- 3 cups milk

Toast bread and cube. Dice potatoes, carrots and celery. Cook in water and soup base. In large bowl, beat eggs; add sage, garlic powder, pepper, chicken broth, melted margarine and onions. When vegetables are done, mix them with egg and spice mixture and add the rest of the ingredients. Grease cake pan with margarine. Bake one hour at 400°.
—Susie Miller, Middleburg IN

3-in-1 Chicken Casserole

- 10 slices toasted bread, cut in 1/2 inch cubes
- 1 cup diced and cooked potatoes
- 1/2 cup diced and cooked carrots
- 1/2 cup diced and cooked celery
- 1 cup cooked chicken
- 6 eggs, well beaten
- 1 pint milk
- 1 cup chicken broth
- 1 teaspoon salt
- 1/2 lb. noodles
- 2 cups chicken broth
- 1/2 cup water
- 1 tablespoon chicken base
- 1/2 teaspoon salt

In large bowl, combine bread cubes, potatoes, carrots, celery and chicken. Beat eggs; add milk, broth and salt. Add to things in bowl. Mix well. Put in well buttered medium-sized roaster. Cook noodles in water about 5 minutes. Drain. Put on top of above mixture. Bring chicken broth, water, chicken base and salt to a boil and thicken with 3/4 cup milk and 4 tablespoons flour. Pour over noodles. Bake at 350° for 1 hour. When about half done baking, put your favorite cheese on top. Serves 10 to 12.
—Betty Miller, Millersburg OH

Don Shenk

Breakfast Casserole

- 6 eggs
- 2 cups milk
- 6 slices bread, cubed
- 1 teaspoon salt
- 1 cup cheese grated
- 1 lb. sausage

Brown sausage and drain. Beat eggs, milk and salt together. Add bread, cheese and sausage. Chill overnight. Bake at 350° for 45 minutes.
—Sarah Miller, Fresno CA

◆ KITCHEN CHAT ◆

DAUGHTER Naomi had supper ready for us when we came in. It was a "haystack supper" consisting of layers of lettuce, noodles, eggs, tomatoes, onions, cheese and crackers, all topped with a cheese sauce.
—Mary Raber, Millersburg, Ohio

Ronald N. Wilson

Upside-Down Pizza

    2 lbs. hamburger *or* sausage
    2 tablespoons chopped onion
    1 pint pizza sauce
Salt and pepper to taste
Pepperoni slices
    3 tablespoons chopped green peppers
    1 small can mushrooms, drained and
      chopped
    1 16-oz. sour cream
Grated mozzarella cheese
    1 can crescent rolls

Fry meat, onion, salt and pepper. Add pizza sauce. Put into the bottom of a 9 x 13 cake pan. Layer with pepperoni, peppers and mushrooms. Bake at 350° for 15 to 20 minutes. Remove from oven and cover with sour cream and mozzarella cheese. Top with crescent rolls and bake at 400° until the rolls are golden brown.
          —*Kathy Miller*
          Millersburg OH

◆ KITCHEN CHAT ◆

YESTERDAY we had church services for 28 families here at our house. We served a light lunch at noon as is custom, consisting of red beets, pickles, bread, strawberry jam, peanut butter, butter, cheese, noodles, coffee and cookies.

    Many years ago, when our country was sparingly settled, the Amish had a long way to travel in horse and buggy for church. So, after the services, a light lunch was served before the long drive home, similar to what we served yesterday. That tradition has been kept on through the years.

    Our 20-year-old daughter, Ruby, and her fiancee, Ora Bontrager, were published for marriage yesterday in church. Lord willing, the wedding will be later this month at our neighbor's, with the reception here at our house.

    Tables will be set up and readied with rented china and silverware for approximately 200 guests. Twenty cooks will prepare two meals, and eight couples will serve the guests.

    Our menu for the wedding dinner is homemade bread, mashed potatoes, dressing, gravy, meat, baked beans, potato salad, a relish tray with celery, carrots and cheese, fruit mixture, butterscotch tortes, cake, pecan and chocolate pies and coffee. Supper will be slightly different.
          —*Edna Miller, Millersburg, Indiana*

Wet Burritos

    1 lb. hamburger
    1 pkg. taco seasoning
    1 can refried beans
    1 16-oz. sour cream
    1 10-oz. can cream of mushroom soup
    1 pkg. tortillas (soft shells)
    1 16 oz. mozzarella cheese, shredded

Brown hamburger. Mix in taco seasoning and refried beans and heat. Mix together sour cream and mushroom soup. Line pan with shells and add a layer of sour cream and soup (about 1/2). Top with meat mixture. Pour on remaining sour cream and soup mixture. Add layer of shells again. Top with cheese and bake until hot, approximately 1/2 hour at 350°.
          —*Laureen Miller, Milford IN*

Haystack

Crushed Ritz *or* soda crackers
Minute rice (3 cups cooked)
Lettuce, cut up
Tomatoes, diced
Hamburger (browned with onions plus 1
    pint pizza sauce to 1 quart hamburger)
Crushed tortilla or corn chips
Cheddar cheese soup (1 can soup diluted
    with 1 can, milk, heated, or you can make
    own cheese sauce)

Put on your plate in layers in the order given, with soup over the top. You'll have a big haystack. Use the amount of each ingredient you prefer.
—*Edna Miller, Guthrie KY*

Lizzie's Meat Loaf

1-1/2 lb. ground beef
  3/4 cup quick rolled oats (uncooked)
  1/4 cup chopped onion
1-1/2 teaspoons salt
  1/4 teaspoon pepper
    1 egg, beaten
  3/4 cup milk

Sauce

1/3 cup catsup
  2 tablespoons brown sugar
  1 tablespoon prepared mustard

Combine all ingredients and mix thoroughly. Pack firmly into a loaf pan. Combine all ingredients for sauce and pour over meat loaf. Bake in preheated 350° oven for 1 hour. Let stand 5 minutes before slicing.   —*Elizabeth Coblentz, Geneva IN*

Sloppy Joes

1 tablespoon shortening
1 large onion, chopped
1 lb. hamburger
1 tablespoon sugar
1 teaspoon salt
1 tablespoon dry mustard
1 green pepper (optional)
Flour
  3/4 cup catsup *or* tomato juice

Fry hamburger and onion in the flour and shortening until brown. Then add the rest of the ingredients to meat mixture and let cook slowly for 1/2 hour before serving.   —*Ada Miller, Utica OH*

Bill Hentosh

Pies

Beatlenut Pie

        3 eggs, well beaten
        1 cup sugar
    1/4 cup margarine, melted
        1 cup milk
        3 tablespoons flour
        1 teaspoon vanilla
    1/4 cup maple syrup
    1/4 cup quick oatmeal
Few pecans, chopped
Sprinkle of coconut
Unbaked pie shell

Combine all ingredients except oatmeal, pecans and coconut. Beat well. Add oatmeal, pecans and coconut. Pour into unbaked pie shell. Bake at 350° about 45 minutes. This pie resembles a custard pie in texture. The coconut, oatmeal and pecans form a crusty topping.   —Susie Beachy, Garnett KS

◆ KITCHEN CHAT ◆

THIS EVENING there were only two eggs in the henhouse. Yesterday all five hens laid.

With tomatoes dwindling down, we fried some for supper, along with milk soup and cinnamon rolls. Later I carried things to the cooler in the basement and put away jars of apple pie filling. We made 60 quarts last week for three families, plus a few to give away.
*   —Miriam Graber, Montgomery, Indiana*

Snow Ghost Cocoa Cream Pie

    1/2 cup cocoa
    1-1/4 cups sugar
    1/3 cup cornstarch
    1/4 teaspoon salt
        2 cups milk
        3 tablespoons butter
    1-1/2 teaspoons vanilla

Combine dry ingredients. Gradually blend in milk, stirring until smooth. Cook over medium heat, stirring constantly until filling boils. Boil 1 minute; remove from heat. Add butter and vanilla. Pour into crust immediately and put waxed paper directly on pie filling so as not to form skin. Refrigerate. Makes one 9-inch pie.
—Ruth Byler, Guys Mills PA

Shoestring Apple Pie

        2 cups white sugar
        2 tablespoons flour
        4 teaspoons water
        3 eggs, beaten
Pinch of salt
        4 cups apples
Cinnamon for top

Combine all ingredients and pour into pie shell. Bake at 375° for one hour or until done.
    —Clara Hershberger, Millersburg OH

Pumpkin Custard Pie

        8 eggs, *separated*
    1-1/2 cups white sugar
    1-1/2 cups brown sugar
        6 tablespoons flour
    1/2 tablespoon pumpkin spice (heaping)
    1/2 teaspoon salt
        1 cup pumpkin
    3/4 cup evaporated milk
    1-1/2 qt. milk, scalded

Separate 4 eggs and set egg whites aside. In a bowl beat 4 eggs plus 4 egg yolks. Add the remaining ingredients except the milk. After milk is heated, add to mixture. Fold in beaten egg whites. Bake at 350° until done. Makes 4 pies.
    —Lorina Miller, Holmersville OH

Pumpkin Pie

    1-1/2 cups cooked pumpkin
        1 cup brown sugar
    1-1/2 cups milk, scalded
        3 eggs, *separated*
    1/2 teaspoon salt
        1 tablespoon cornstarch
    1/4 teaspoon ginger
    1/4 teaspoon cloves
        1 teaspoon cinnamon

Cook pumpkin. Rub through sieve. Add beaten egg yolks, sugar, salt and spices. Gradually add milk and mix thoroughly. Fold in beaten egg whites. Pour into an unbaked crust. Bake at 425° for 10 minutes, reduce heat to 350° and bake 30 minutes more. Makes one 9-inch pie.
    —Ruth Hershberger, Milroy IN

Shoo Fly Pie

Filling

>   1 egg, well beaten
>   1 tablespoon flour (heaping)
>   1 cup maple syrup
>   1 cup brown sugar
>   2 cups cold water
>   1 teaspoon vanilla

Pinch of salt

Mix together egg, flour, syrup, brown sugar and water; heat to boiling. Cool. Add vanilla. Pour into 2 unbaked pie shells.

Topping

>   2 cups flour
>   1/2 cup brown sugar
>   1 teaspoon baking soda
>   1 teaspoon cream of tartar
>   1/2 cup shortening *or* butter

Mix together flour, sugar, baking soda and cream of tartar. Add shortening or butter. Sprinkle over top of pie mixture. Bake for 30 minutes at 375°.

—*Barbara Miller, Lyles TN*

Sour Cream Pecan Pie

>   3 eggs
>   1/2 cup sour cream
>   1/2 cup dark corn syrup
>   1 teaspoon vanilla
>   1 cup sugar
>   1/8 teaspoon salt
>   2 tablespoons butter, melted
> 1-1/4 cups pecans
>   1 unbaked 9-inch pie shell

Bake in preheated 400° oven until crust is brown and filling is slightly puffy (30 to 35 minutes).

—*Naomi Mast, Mondovi WI*

Apple Pie

Apples for one pie
>   1 cup brown sugar
>   2 tablespoons minute tapioca

Water (enough to make syrup-type juice)
Pinch of salt
Cinnamon
>   3 dabs butter

Use any kind of pie pastry you wish. Have enough dough for a full crust on top. Wet the bottom crust on outer edge to make the two stick together when you pinch the edges together. Peel and chop apples. Add brown sugar, tapioca, water, salt and cinnamon. Put 3 dabs of butter in bottom crust to prevent juice running out of pan. Bake at 450° until apples cook through. Wet the top crust with cream or milk and sprinkle white sugar over it and bake until a golden brown.

—*Ella Herschberger, Pardeeville WI*

Cottage Pie

Crust

>   6 cups flour
>   2 cups shortening
>   1 teaspoon salt

Mix and add enough water to form dough. Makes three 9-inch pie shells.

Filling

>   1 cup sugar
>   1 cup maple syrup
>   1 egg
>   1 pint water
>   1 tablespoon flour
>   1 tablespoon vanilla

Topping

>   2 cups sugar
>   1 egg
>   1 cup shortening
>   1 cup sour milk
>   1 teaspoon baking soda
>   3 cups flour

Mix bottom ingredients together and bring to a boil. Set aside. Cream sugar and shortening. Add egg, milk and stir. Finally, add flour and baking soda. Pour filling into pie shells. Place topping over filling by dropping with teaspoon until all is used. Bake at 375° for about 45 minutes.

—*Martha Miller*
Mesopotamia OH

◆ ◆ ◆

◆◆◆

Coconut Nut Cream Pie

    2 cups milk
    2 egg yolks
  2/3 cup sugar
    1 tablespoon flour
    1 tablespoon cornstarch
  1/2 teaspoon salt
    1 teaspoon vanilla
  1/2 cup coconut
  1/2 cup chopped nuts

Heat milk and sugar to boiling point and thicken with mixture of flour, cornstarch, egg yolks and salt. When cool, add vanilla, coconut and nuts. Top with whipped cream. —Ira Miller, Fredonia PA

Pumpkin Pie

Crust

    3 cups flour
  1-1/2 teaspoons baking powder
  1-1/2 teaspoons white sugar
  1/2 teaspoon salt
    1 cup lard *or* shortening (butter flavor)
    1 egg yolk, beaten (in a cup filled half full with water)

Mix lard with dry ingredients until crumbly. Add water and egg and mix well. Makes crusts for 2 pies.

Filling

  1-1/2 cups brown sugar
    1 tablespoon flour
    1 cup mashed pumpkin
    2 teaspoons pumpkin pie spice
    5 eggs, *separated*
  1/2 teaspoon salt
    2 teaspoons vanilla
    3 cups milk, scalded

Mix in order given, the hot milk last. Add egg whites and beat together. Bake at 400° for 10 minutes. Reduce to 350° and bake for 30 minutes.
—Frieda Mast, Millersburg OH

◆◆◆

Swedish Apple Pie

- 1 can (30 oz.) apple pie filling
- 1 cup flour
- 2/3 cup sugar
- 1 teaspoon baking powder
- 1/4 teaspoon salt
- 1/2 cup butter *or* margarine
- 1 egg slightly beaten
- 1/2 cup chopped walnuts

Spread pie filling smoothly into an oiled pan. In a mixing bowl, stir together flour, sugar, baking powder and salt. Blend in softened butter and egg, stirring to make a thick batter. Drop batter from spoon to cover pie filling. Sprinkle with nuts. Bake at 350° for 45 minutes or until apples are bubbly and topping is nicely brown. Serve warm with dollops of whipped topping or ice cream. (Cherry or blueberry pie filling can be substituted.) This can make two 8-inch pies, one deep dish 10-inch pie or one 9 x 9 x 2 inch dessert. —*Mary Ann Miller Baltic OH*

Ronald N. Wilson

French Rhubarb Pie

Filling

- 1 egg
- 1 cup sugar
- 1 teaspoon vanilla
- 2 cups diced rhubarb
- 2 tablespoons flour

Topping

- 3/4 cup flour
- 1/2 cup brown sugar
- 1/3 cup butter

Mix filling ingredients together and pour into an unbaked pie shell. Cover with topping. Bake at 400° for 10 minutes. Continue baking at 350° for 30 minutes or until done. —*Susan Miller Millersburg OH*

Deluxe Pecan Pie

- 3 eggs
- 1 cup light corn syrup
- 3/4 cup white sugar
- 2 tablespoons butter, melted
- 1 teaspoon salt
- 1 cup chopped pecans

In medium-size bowl, beat eggs well. Add corn syrup, sugar, melted butter and salt. Put pecans in bottom of unbaked pie shell. Pour egg mixture over pecans. Bake for 60 minutes at 350° or until knife inserted comes out clean. —*Elsie Yoder Sugar Creek OH*

◆ KITCHEN CHAT ◆

I CANNED some pickled red beets today and also prepared a butternut squash from the garden, which will be good to bake a few pies whenever I find time, perhaps tomorrow.

For dinner we had mashed potatoes, creamed chicken, buttered red beets, applesauce, peaches and coconut cake.

After school, grandchildren Japheth and Rose Mary picked some peppermint and spearmint tea leaves for me to dry for tea in the cold winter days ahead. Usually when they do an errand for me, I throw a little snack party, with sometimes a game of Rummycube included.

—Mary Schlabach, Millersburg, Ohio

Pumpkin Chiffon Pie

Crust

- 2 cups shortening
- 1/4 cup vinegar
- 1 egg
- 1 cup water
- 1/4 teaspoon salt
- 1/4 teaspoon baking soda
- 5 cups flour

In a bowl, mix shortening, vinegar and egg. Add water, salt and baking soda. Blend in flour.

Filling

- 1 tablespoon unflavored gelatin
- 2/3 cup packed brown sugar
- 1/2 teaspoon salt
- 1/2 teaspoon nutmeg
- 1/2 teaspoon cinnamon
- 1-1/4 cups cooked and mashed pumpkin
- 3 eggs, *separated*
- 1/2 cup sugar

Cook gelatin, brown sugar, spices, pumpkin and 3 egg yolks over medium heat, stirring constantly until it boils. Remove from heat and cool. Carefully fold in 3 egg whites beaten stiffly with sugar. Pour into baked pie crust. Chill until set (2 hours). Top with whipped cream.
— *Vera Jess*
Arthur IL

Shoestring Apple Pie

- 2 cups white sugar
- 1 tablespoon flour
- 4 eggs, well beaten
- 1 cup milk
- 5 cups shredded apples

Pinch of salt
- 1 teaspoon vanilla

Mix all together. Pour into an unbaked pie shell. Sprinkle cinnamon over top. Bake at 350° for 30 minutes or until done. Makes two pies.
— *Maudie Raber, Millersburg OH*

Shoo Fly Pie

Filling

- 1 cup sugar
- 1 cup dark syrup
- 1 pint water
- 1 tablespoon flour (heaping)
- 1 egg beaten
- 1 teaspoon vanilla

Boil above until thick. Let cool. Place in unbaked pie crust.

Crumb Topping

- 1/2 cup sugar
- 2 cups flour
- 1/2 cup lard
- 1 teaspoon baking soda
- 1 teaspoon cream of tartar

Mix together and put on top of pie filling.
— *Mrs. Samuel Mast, Bruceton TN*

Fruit Pizza

Crust

>   1/2 cup butter
>   1/4 cup brown sugar
>   1 egg
> 1-1/3 cups flour
>   1 teaspoon baking powder

Pinch of salt

Cream together butter, sugar and egg. Add baking powder and salt. Press in a greased pizza pan and bake for 10 minutes at 375°.

Filling

>   8 oz. cream cheese
> 1/2 teaspoon vanilla
> 1/2 cup powdered sugar
> 1/4 cup whipped cream

Apples, grapes, oranges, kiwis, bananas, strawberries, pineapple or any fresh fruit can be used. Arrange in circles on baked crust.

Topping

>   2 cups fruit juice (any kind)
> 1/2 cup sugar
>   1 tablespoon clear gelatin
>   2 tablespoons Jell-O (any kind)

Cook above ingredients until clear. Cool and dribble over fruit. Serve. May also be topped with whipped cream.   —*Katie Yoder, St. Mary's ON*

Pumpkin Pie

>   1 pint pumpkin
>   3 cups sugar
>   6 tablespoons flour
>   6 eggs, *separated*
>   1 teaspoon cinnamon
>   1 teaspoon pumpkin pie spice
>   3 cups milk

Dash of salt

Combine all ingredients except egg whites. Beat egg whites until stiff and fold into mixture. Pour in pie shells and bake at 350° until set. Makes 3 pies.
—*Margaret Troyer, Smicksburg PA*

◆ KITCHEN CHAT ◆

AFTER finishing with the washing, I stirred up a batch of bread dough and set the cream out of the refrigerator to warm up a bit before churning.

The three youngest girls and I had lunch of baked buttercup squash with chicken gravy, lettuce sandwiches, vegetable stew, fresh tomatoes and red peppers, sauerkraut and Concord grapes.

This afternoon I cleaned and cut the rhubarb my husband, Marvin, brought in before leaving for work. I made a rhubarb crunch and then churned 3 pounds of butter.

—*Anna Marie Yoder, Scottville, Michigan*

Ronald N. Wilson

Peach Pie

Filling

6 peaches, sliced
1 unbaked pie shell
1/4 cup flour
3/4 cup sugar
1 cup sweet cream

Arrange peaches in pie shell. Mix flour, sugar and cream. Pour over peaches.

Topping

1/3 cup flour
1/3 cup sugar
3 tablespoons butter

Combine above ingredients and put over pie filling. Bake at 425° for 10 minutes. Reduce heat to 350° and bake until custard is set (about 30 minutes).
—Katie Zook, Apple Creek OH

Old-Fashioned Cream Pie

Crust

1 cup flour
1/3 cup vegetable oil
3 tablespoons milk
Sprinkle of salt

Mix ingredients in a pie pan. Pat around edges with fingers.

Filling

2/3 cup white sugar
1/3 cup brown sugar

1 tablespoon flour (heaping)
Pinch of salt
1 teaspoon vanilla
1 cup cream
2 eggs, *separated*

Mix brown sugar and egg yolks. Add the remaining ingredients with egg whites last. Bake at 350° for 45 minutes. —Edna Miller, Millersburg IN

Amish Shoefly Pie

Syrup Mixture

1 cup molasses
1/2 cup brown sugar
2 eggs, lightly beaten
1 cup hot water
1 teaspoon baking soda, dissolved in hot water

Mix syrup ingredients thoroughly together. Pour into two 8-inch unbaked pie shells. Put crumb mixture on top of syrup. Bake at 400° for 10 minutes. Reduce heat to 350° and continue baking for 50 minutes. Let cool.

Crumb Mixture

2 cups flour
3/4 cup brown sugar
1/3 cup lard *or* oleo
1/2 teaspoon cinnamon

Mix above ingredients together thoroughly until crumbs form. —Mary Yoder, Fredericksburg OH

Apple Pie

Filling

4 cups chopped apples
3/4 cup cream
1/4 teaspoon salt
1/4 cup flour
3/4 cup white sugar

Topping

1/4 cup brown sugar
1 teaspoon cinnamon

Combine apples and dry ingredients and mix well. Blend in cream. Place in an unbaked pie shell. Sprinkle with topping and bake for 15 minutes at 450°. Reduce heat to 350° and continue baking until done. —Eldon Ropp, Bremen IN

Jonas Coblentz

Desserts

Carrot Cake

    2 cups sugar
    4 eggs
    2 teaspoons baking soda
    2 teaspoons baking powder
    3 cups grated raw carrots
 1-1/2 cups cooking oil
    2 cups flour
    1 teaspoon salt
    2 teaspoons cinnamon
  1/2 cup chopped nuts

Cream sugar and cooking oil. Add eggs. Sift flour, baking powder and cinnamon together. Add to cream mixture. Add salt and baking soda. Fold in carrots and nuts. Bake in loaf pan at 350°.
                    —Verna Bylers, Lucknow ON

Our Family's Favorite Dessert

    4 cups sugar
    4 cups flour
    3 cups milk
    2 teaspoons salt
    4 teaspoons baking powder
    4 tablespoons butter
    4 tablespoons baking cocoa
    4 eggs

Mix all ingredients and bake.
                    —Barbara Byler, Marion KY

Easy Cream Cheese Squares

    1 cup sugar, *divided*
  1/3 cup butter
 1-1/2 cups graham cracker crumbs
    3 8-oz. pkgs. cream cheese
    4 eggs, beaten
    1 teaspoon vanilla
    1 21-oz. can blueberry *or* raspberry
      pie filling

Preheat oven to 325°. In a saucepan heat the butter and 1/4 cup sugar until melted, stirring occasionally. Add graham cracker crumbs. Press in 9 x 13 baking pan. With an electric mixer, beat cream cheese until smooth. Gradually beat in remaining sugar. Add one egg at a time; then vanilla and blend well. Spoon blueberry fill over crust.

Carefully pour cream cheese mixture over blueberry filling. Bake until set, 45 to 50 minutes. Chill; cut in squares.   —*Mary Beachy, Baltic OH*

Revel Bars

    2 sticks butter
    2 cups brown sugar
    2 eggs
  1/2 teaspoon salt
    1 teaspoon baking soda
    3 cups oatmeal
 2-1/2 cups flour

Filling

    2 cups chocolate chips *or*
      butterscotch chips
    2 cans condensed milk
    1 tablespoon butter
Sprinkle of salt

Mix and put one half of dough in 9 x 13 pan. Melt filling in a double boiler. Spread filling over dough and put rest of dough on top.   —*Ruth Byler Guys Mills PA*

◆ KITCHEN CHAT ◆

MOM, Naomi, Elizabeth and Mary went over to Enoch Byler's to help get ready for church.

   We are having a surprise birthday party for Mom tomorrow night, so I was glad she went away so I could get some food ready. I quickly baked two treats, Revel Bars and Blind Date Loaf. Soon as they were done baking, I hid them in my buggy.

   Wouldn't you believe, when Mom came home she wanted to bake some bars. I knew she would want to use the same pans that I had used for my treats, so I grabbed a bowl and ran out the back door to the buggy.

   I hastily put the bars in the bowl, then ran to the milkhouse and washed the pans there. While I was still in the milkhouse, Mom asked Elizabeth, "Where are my cake pans?"

   While they were hunting, I came in the back door and put them on the counter. Wow! That was close!
                    —*Ruth Byler, Guys Mills, Pennsylvania*

◆ KITCHEN CHAT ◆

AFTER our breakfast of scrambled eggs, tomato gravy, cornflakes and doughnuts, it was a scramble to get the dishes washed, floors swept and husband Harvey (a teacher) and five older children off to school.

Now I'm left alone with our three little boys, ages 1, 2 and 4, wondering what I will get done till the others come home again.

Those little ones can at times keep me pretty busy. I decided to work inside in the forenoon while I baked bread, since one of the girls had made dough before she went to school. While it baked, I put a "Trip Around the World" wall hanger quilt in frame.

Our 4-year-old was coloring a picture in his book, and the little ones got hold of some colors. One of them came to the kitchen and said, "Color gute", which means good. I saw traces of it around his mouth!

Later, two of the children went outside to play. When dinner was ready, I went to get them in. I found them up in the barn sitting on a pile of cow feed! They both looked as dusty as little feed bags!

—Ada Miller, Utica, Ohio

Cinnamon Rolls

- **1 cake *or* tablespoon yeast**
- **1 cup warm water**
- **1/2 teaspoon salt**
- **5 tablespoons sugar, *divided***
- **6 cups flour, *divided***
- **2 cups milk, scalded**
- **2 eggs, well beaten**
- **1/2 cup butter, melted**

Filling

- **4 tablespoons sugar**
- **4 tablespoons butter**
- **1-1/2 teaspoons cinnamon**
- **1/4 cup chopped nuts**

Soften yeast in warm water and add salt, 1 tablespoon of sugar and enough flour (about 2 cups) to make a dough. Let rise one hour. Add cooled milk, eggs, butter, remaining sugar and more flour to make a soft dough. Let rise again. Roll out on floured board. To prepare filling: Mix sugar, butter, cinnamon and nuts together with a fork. Spread on dough. Roll up like a jelly roll and cut crosswise into 2-inch pieces. Place in a greased pan, cut side up. Let rise until double in size and bake at 400° for 20 minutes. Makes 18 large rolls.—*Lydia Mast, Meyersdale PA*

Butterscotch Tapioca

- 6 cups boiling water
- 1 teaspoon salt
- 1-1/2 cups pearl tapioca (has to be pearl)
- 2 cups brown sugar
- 2 eggs, beaten
- 1 cup milk
- 1/2 cup white sugar
- 1 stick butter
- 1 teaspoon vanilla

Cool Whip
Bananas
Snickers candy bars

In a saucepan, boil water, salt and tapioca. Cook for 15 minutes. Add brown sugar. Cook until tapioca pearls are clear, stirring often. Mix together and add eggs, milk and white sugar. Cook again until it bubbles. Brown and add butter and vanilla. Cool and add Cool Whip, bananas and diced Snickers candy bars. —*Esther Christner Shipshewana IN*

John L. Randolph

◆ KITCHEN CHAT ◆

WHEN I went to start lunch, I discovered we were out of propane. No hot water...and the refrigerator was off, too!

Luckily, we use an old kitchen wood stove for heat.
—*Sarah Coblentz, Farwell, Michigan*

Pumpkin Pudding Dessert

Crust

- 1 cup flour
- 1 cup coconut
- 1/2 cup oleo *or* shortening

Press in bottom of 9 x 13 pan and bake 10 minutes at 350°.

Pudding

- 4 cups pumpkin
- 1-1/2 cups sugar
- 4 eggs
- 1/2 cup milk
- 1 teaspoon vanilla
- 2 teaspoons cinnamon

While crust is baking, mix pudding in order given. Pour over crust and bake at 350° for 40 to 50 minutes. —*Mary Ellen Gingerich, Kalona IA*

Blind Date Loaf Cake

- 1/2 cup shortening
- 1 cup sugar
- 2 eggs
- 1 teaspoon vanilla
- 1-1/4 cups flour
- 1/2 teaspoon salt
- 3 teaspoons cocoa
- 1 box of dates
- 1-1/4 cups boiling water
- 1 teaspoon baking soda

Cream shortening and sugar. Add eggs and vanilla; mix well. Sift dry ingredients together and add to creamed mixture. Mix together dates, baking soda and water; fold into batter Cool. Put in 9 x 13 pan.

Topping

- 6 oz. chocolate chips
- 1/2 cup sugar
- 1/2 cup chopped nuts

Sprinkle over top lightly. Bake at 350° for 35 to 40 minutes. —*Ruth Byler, Guys Mills PA*

Don Shenk

Apple Crunch

   6 cups sliced apples
3/4 cup all-purpose flour
3/4 cup oatmeal, uncooked
1/4 teaspoon nutmeg
1/2 cup butter

Cook apple slices until soft and thick (with a little cornstarch and sweetened to suit your taste). Put this in a cake pan. Combine the remaining ingredients and spread on top of apples. Bake until brown. Serve warm with milk if desired.

—Dora Hostetler, Mt. Victory OH

Apple Dapple

   2 eggs
   2 cups white sugar
   1 cup cooking oil
   3 cups flour (scant)
1/2 teaspoon salt
   1 teaspoon baking soda
   2 teaspoons vanilla
   3 cups chopped apples

Nuts

Mix together eggs, sugar and cooking oil. Sift together flour, salt and baking soda and add to above mixture. Finally, add vanilla, apples and nuts. Pour into a greased pan. Bake 45 minutes at 350°.

Icing

   1 cup brown sugar
1/4 cup milk
1/4 cup oil

Combine and cook 2-1/2 minutes. Stir a little after removing from heat, but do not beat. Dribble over cake while icing and cake are still warm.

—Miriam Bontrager, Wolcottville IN

Cream-Filled Coffee Cake

3/4 cup milk
1/3 cup water
1/4 cup sugar
   1 stick margarine
1-1/2 teaspoons salt
   2 eggs, beaten
   4 cups flour
1-1/2 tablespoons instant yeast

Crumbs

1/2 cup brown sugar
1/4 cup flour
1/4 teaspoon cinnamon
1/4 stick oleo, firm

Filling

4-2/3 cups powdered sugar
   2 egg whites, stiffly beaten
3/4 cup shortening
1/2 teaspoon salt
   2 teaspoons vanilla
1/3 cup water

Heat milk and water to scalding. Add the sugar, margarine and salt. Have milk at least 120°. Add eggs, flour and yeast. Work dough, adding more flour as needed. Have dough slightly sticky. Let rise for 1 hour, then work out into four greased pie or round cake pans. Put crumbs on top and let rise again until double. Bake at 350° for 10 to 15 minutes. When cakes are cooled, remove from pans and cut off tops. Spread filling on lower half and replace top half. *—Ann Knepp, Haven KS*

Pistachio Delight

- 1 cup chopped walnuts
- 2 cups flour
- 1 cup soft margarine *or* butter

Mix all together until crumbs. Put in 9 x 13 pan. Press evenly. Bake at 350° for 15 minutes. Cool.

- 4 oz. cream cheese
- 1 cup powdered sugar
- 1 cup Cool Whip

Cream together the above and spread over baked crust.

- 2 3-1/2-oz. boxes instant pistachio pudding
- 2-3/4 cups cold milk
- 1 teaspoon vanilla

Nuts

Mix above together and beat for 2 minutes. Spread over top of cream cheese mixture. Cover with Cool Whip and garnish with chopped nuts. Chill.

—Sarah Coblentz, Farwell MI

Homemade Ice Cream

- 2-1/2 cups milk, *divided*
- 1 tablespoon cornstarch
- 1 tablespoon flour
- 1/2 cup brown sugar
- 1 teaspoon vanilla
- 4 eggs
- 4 cups sugar
- 1-1/2 quarts cream

Cook 2 cups of milk over low heat and bring to a boil. Mix together cornstarch, flour, brown sugar, vanilla, eggs and 1/2 cup milk. Add to the boiling milk and cook until thick. Blend in sugar and cream and enough milk to fill a 6-quart freezer can. It takes 25 lbs. of ice and 3/4 quart salt to freeze a 6 quart freezer. Usually takes about 25 minutes to freeze or when you can't turn it anymore.

—Edna Helmuth, Evansville WI

Caramel Pear Pudding Cake

- 1 cup all-purpose flour
- 2/3 cup sugar
- 1-1/2 teaspoons baking powder
- 1/2 teaspoon cinnamon
- 1/4 teaspoon salt

Dash ground cloves

- 1/2 cup milk
- 2 cups chopped pears
- 1/2 cup chopped pecans
- 3/4 cup brown sugar
- 1/4 cup butter *or* margarine
- 3/4 cup boiling water

Mix together flour, sugar, baking powder, cinnamon, salt and cloves. Add milk; beat until smooth. Stir in pears and pecans. Turn into an ungreased 2-quart casserole. In a separate bowl, combine brown sugar, butter or margarine, and boiling water. Pour evenly over batter. Bake at 375° for 45 minutes. Delicious with ice cream, whipped cream or just plain milk. Can also be made with apples.

—Sarah Hertzler, Elkhart Lake WI

Ronald N. Wilson

Squash Cake

- 3 eggs
- 2 cups cooked and mashed winter squash
- 1 cup oil
- 2 cups sugar
- 2 cups flour
- 2 teaspoons baking powder
- 2 teaspoons baking soda
- 2 teaspoons cinnamon
- 1/2 teaspoon salt

Combine eggs, squash and oil and beat well. Add the remaining ingredients. Bake at 350° until done.
—*Miriam Graber, Montgomery IN*

Cinnamon Rolls

- 1-1/2 cups milk
- 1/2 cup sugar
- 1/2 cup margarine
- 2 pkg. yeast
- 1/2 cup lukewarm water
- 3 eggs, beaten
- 6 cups flour
- Brown sugar
- Cinnamon

Scald milk and add sugar and margarine. Mix the yeast and water and let stand 5 minutes. Add to above mixture. Then add the eggs and 3 cups of the flour. Mix in remaining flour and let rise until double in size. Roll out and spread with melted margarine. Sprinkle brown sugar and cinnamon on top. Roll up. Cut about 3/4 to 1 inch thick slices. Let rise. Bake in hot oven 5 to 7 minutes. Frost them when out of the oven.   —*Elizabeth Coblentz*
Geneva IN

Rhoda's Apple Rollups

Dough

- 2 cups flour
- 2-1/2 teaspoons baking powder
- 1/2 teaspoon salt
- 2/3 cup shortening
- 1/2 cup milk
- 6 apples, peeled
- 1/2 cup brown sugar
- 1/2 teaspoon cinnamon

Sauce

- 2 cups brown sugar
- 2 cups water
- 1/4 cup butter
- 1/2 teaspoon cinnamon

Mix flour, baking powder, salt, shortening and milk. Roll out dough, as a jelly roll. Dice apples and spread over dough. After it has been spread with butter, sprinkle with brown sugar and cinnamon. Roll up and cut like rolls. Place in cake pan so they do not touch. Pour on the sauce and bake at 375° for 35 to 40 minutes. Serve hot with vanilla ice cream or cold milk.   —*Rebecca Schwartz*
Norfolk NY

Date Pudding

- 1 cup chopped dates
- 1 teaspoon baking soda
- 1 cup hot water
- 1 cup brown sugar
- 1 tablespoon butter
- 1 cup flour
- 1 egg

Pour hot water over dates and baking soda and let stand until cool. Add brown sugar, butter, flour and egg. Bake at 350° in a cake pan. When cold, or next day, cut in small pieces and put in layers in a dish with whipped cream, drizzling it with caramel sauce.

Caramel Sauce

- 1 tablespoon butter, browned
- 3/4 cup brown sugar
- 1 cup water
- 1 tablespoon clear gelatin
- 1 teaspoon vanilla

Heat butter, brown sugar and water to boiling and thicken with clear gelatin. Add the vanilla.
—*Edna Schlabach, Dundee OH*

Topping for Angel Food Cake

- 2 boxes instant vanilla pudding
- 3 cups milk
- 1 8-oz. pkg. cream cheese, softened
- 1 can crushed pineapple, drained
- 1 small container of Cool Whip

Mix instant pudding and milk together. Add the cream cheese. Stir in pineapple and Cool Whip. Serve on individual slices of angel food cake.
—*Mrs. Melvin Miller, Sugar Creek OH*

◆ KITCHEN CHAT ◆
THIS AFTERNOON I picked grapes and made them into grape juice, getting the shelves filled for the winter season. On cold winter evenings, popcorn and grape juice is a real treat!
—*Mattie Yoder, Millersburg, Ohio*

Roman Apple Cake

- 1 cup shortening
- 1 cup white sugar
- 1/2 cup brown sugar
- 2 eggs
- 2-1/2 cups flour
- 1 teaspoon baking soda
- 1 teaspoon baking powder
- 1 teaspoon cinnamon
- 1/2 teaspoon salt
- 1 cup chopped apples
- 1 cup sour milk

Topping

- 1/2 cup white sugar
- 1 teaspoon cinnamon

Cream together shortening and sugars. Add remaining ingredients. Sprinkle topping over batter. Bake at 325° for 35 to 40 minutes. Stick a toothpick down into top in several places so it won't just form a crust and not bake through. —*Beverly Miller, Bloomfield IA*

Doyle Yoder

Large Chocolate Cake

        2 cups raw *or* brown sugar
      3/4 cup oil
        2 eggs, beaten
    2-1/2 cups flour
      1/2 cup cocoa
        1 cup buttermilk *or* sour milk
        1 teaspoon vanilla
      1/2 teaspoon salt
        2 teaspoons baking soda

Chocolate Nut Icing

    3-1/2 cups powder sugar, sifted
      1/2 cup butter, softened
        3 tablespoons cocoa
        1 teaspoon vanilla
      1/2 teaspoon salt
      1/4 cup milk
      3/4 cup chopped nuts

Cream together sugar and shortening. Add eggs and mix well. To this mixture, add alternately the flour, which has been sifted once with the cocoa, and sour milk. Mix carefully. Add salt and vanilla. Finally, stir in a little boiling water in which you have dissolved the baking soda. Bake at 325° for 30 to 45 minutes. When cake is done, put 2 cups of miniature marshmallows on top. Return to the oven for 2 minutes. Ice with Chocolate Nut Icing.
—*Lizzie Schlabach, Dunnville KY*

Baked Apple Dessert

        5 cups water
    1-1/2 cups brown sugar
      1/2 teaspoon cinnamon
        6 large apples
Gelatin *or* cornstarch

Dissolve sugar in water and bring to a boil. Thicken with clear gelatin or cornstarch. Add cinnamon. Peel apples and cut into halves. Put the apples in a 9 x 13 baking dish and pour sugar and water mixture over apples. Bake for 1-1/2 hours at 350°. Top with whipped topping. Serve hot or cold.
—*Edna Miller, Fredericksburg OH*

◆ *KITCHEN CHAT* ◆

SUPPER consisted of macaroni and cheese, three-in-one gravy and cornbread, plus raspberry tapioca.

After the dishes were washed, we hitched the two horses to the double buggy and went for groceries. We got eggs at Grandpa Herschberger's and sugar at Felty Herschberger's, then stopped at Mishler's Country Store for bulk foods.

By the time we got home it was 9:30 p.m. and we were all tired and ready for bed.
—*Mrs. Floyd Herschberger*
Pardeeville, Wisconsin

Strawberry Delight

    2 cups crushed pretzels
    3 tablespoons sugar
  3/4 cup butter *or* oleo
    8 oz. cream cheese
  3/4 cup powdered sugar
    2 cups marshmallows
    1 pkg. Dream Whip, whipped
    1 6-oz. strawberry Jell-O
2-1/2 cups hot water
    1 quart frozen strawberries

Combine pretzels, sugar and melted butter. Press into a 9 x 13 pan and bake at 350° for 15 minutes. Let cool. Cream the powdered sugar, marshmallows and cream cheese together. Add Dream Whip. Spread on top of pretzel layer. Dissolve strawberry Jell-O in water and add strawberries. Stir this together and let it get kind of thick. Place on top of white mixture and let set.

—Laureen Miller, Milford IN

Cream-Filled Coffee Cake

    1 cup milk, scalded
  1/2 cup white sugar
  1/2 cup oleo
    1 teaspoon salt
    2 eggs, beaten
    1 pkg. dry yeast
  1/4 cup warm water
3-1/2 cups bread flour

Crumbs

  1/2 cup brown sugar
  1/2 cup flour
  1/4 cup butter
    1 teaspoon cinnamon

Filling

    3 egg whites
    3 cups powdered sugar
1-1/2 cups shortening
    3 teaspoons vanilla
  1/4 cup milk

Combine milk, white sugar, oleo and salt. Add eggs and stir. Dissolve dry yeast in warm water and add to above. Blend in flour and let rise in refrigerator overnight. Next morning, put dough in four greased pie pans. Spread crumbs on top and let rise until double. Bake at 350° for 25 minutes. Cool and split each and fill.

—Katie Troyer
Fredericksburg OH

Apple Dumplings

    6 apples, peeled and halved

Dough

    2 cups pastry flour
2-1/2 teaspoons baking powder
  1/2 teaspoon salt
  2/3 cup shortening
  1/2 cup milk

Sauce

    2 cups brown sugar
    2 cups water
  1/4 cup butter *or* oleo
  1/2 teaspoon cinnamon

Mix flour, baking powder, salt and shortening like pie dough. Add milk. Roll out dough and cut in squares. Place 1/2 apple on each square. Wet edges of dough and press into a ball around apple. Set dumplings in a greased pan. Bring sauce ingredients to a boil. Pour over dumplings. Bake at 350° for 35 minutes or until apples test tender.

—Mary Ann Miller, Baltic OH

Velvet Angel Food Cake

1-2/3 cups egg whites
1 cup sugar
1 teaspoon vanilla
1-1/4 cups cake flour
1-1/3 cups powdered sugar
1-1/2 teaspoons cream of tartar
1/4 teaspoon salt

Beat egg whites until stiff peaks form. Gradually add sugar and vanilla. Fold flour, powdered sugar, cream of tartar and salt into egg whites by adding a few tablespoons at a time. Bake at 350° for about 45 minutes or until done.

—Annabelle Schmucker, Quincy IL

Fluffy Tapioca Pudding

1 quart milk
1/2 cup tapioca (not minute)
1/2 cup sugar
1/4 teaspoon salt
3 egg yolks, beaten
1-1/2 teaspoons vanilla
1 8-oz. Cool Whip
1 or 2 Snickers candy bars, chopped

Combine milk, tapioca, sugar and salt; let set for 5 minutes. Slowly stir in egg yolks. Bring to a boil, stirring constantly. When it boils, keep on very low heat, stirring occasionally until tapioca is fully cooked. Remove from heat and add vanilla. When cool, stir in Cool Whip and Snickers candy bars.

—Lena Helmuth, Rosebush MI

Spotted Cake

1/2 teaspoon salt
1 cup lard
4 cups flour
2 cups sugar
2 tablespoons cocoa
1 teaspoon cinnamon
2 cups sour milk
2 teaspoons soda

With salt, lard and flour, mix as pie dough. Add sugar, cocoa, cinnamon, sour milk and soda. Mix, but not thoroughly. Leave some of the pie dough chunks in the mixture. Bake. *—Lydia Schwartz Montgomery MI*

Ann's Chocolate Cake

3/4 cup cocoa
1-1/2 cups boiling water
3/4 cup margarine
1-1/2 cups sugar
3 eggs
1-1/2 teaspoons vanilla
1-1/2 teaspoons soda
1-1/2 teaspoons baking powder
1/2 teaspoon salt
2-1/4 cups flour

Mix cocoa and boiling water and set aside. Cream together margarine, sugar, eggs and vanilla. Add dry ingredients alternately with cocoa and water mixture. Mix very well. Put in greased 9 x 13 pan and bake at 350° for 30 to 35 minutes or until toothpick stuck in middle comes out dry.

—Fannie Miller, Sears MI

Ronald N. Wilson

Marvin Yoder

Nut Roll Candy

- 1 cup brown sugar
- 2 cups white sugar
- 1/3 cup butter
- 1 cup white syrup
- 1 cup sweet cream
- 1 cup nut meats

Cook until it forms a hard ball in cold water. Remove from stove and pour nut meats in while hot.

Stir until cool. Pour on buttered platter. Knead into a cream roll and cut into desired slices.

—Barbara Byler, Marion KY

Fruit Pizza

- 1-1/2 cups flour
- 1-1/2 teaspoons baking powder
- 1/2 cup sugar
- 1-1/2 teaspoons vanilla
- 1-1/2 tablespoons milk
- 8 oz. cream cheese
- 1 cup powdered sugar
- 1/2 cup milk
- 1 small box instant vanilla pudding
- 1 small container whipped topping

Topping

- 2 tablespoons strawberry gelatin
- 2 tablespoons sugar
- 1 tablespoon clear gelatin
- 3/4 cup water

Mix flour, baking powder, sugar, vanilla and milk like a pie crust and press into a pizza pan. Bake for 10 minutes at 350°. Cool. Mix cream cheese, powdered sugar, milk and vanilla pudding together. Add whipped topping and spread over cooled crust. Top with any kind of fruit you may have on hand. Cook topping ingredients until thick. Cool and pour over fruit.

—Mary Raber
Millersburg OH

Pine Scotch Pudding

    3/4 cup flour
      1 teaspoon baking powder
    1/4 teaspoon salt
      2 eggs
      1 cup sugar
      1 teaspoon vanilla
      1 cup drained pineapple
      1 cup chopped nuts

Sift together flour, baking powder and salt. Beat eggs until fluffy. Gradually add sugar, beating constantly until thick and ivory colored. Add vanilla, pineapple and chopped nuts. Fold in dry ingredients gently but thoroughly. Bake in slow oven 30 to 35 minutes. Cool; cut in squares. Serve with whipped cream and butterscotch sauce.

Butterscotch Sauce

    1/4 cup butter *or* margarine
      1 tablespoon flour
      1 cup firmly packed brown sugar
    1/4 cup pineapple juice
    1/4 cup water
      1 egg, beaten

Melt butter in saucepan and stir in flour. Add brown sugar, pineapple juice and water. Mix well and boil for 3 minutes, stirring constantly. Blend in egg to which a little of the hot sauce has been added. Cook 1 minute and add vanilla. *—Elizabeth Miller Cashton WI*

Oh Henry Bars

      1 cup sugar
      1 cup white Karo
    1-1/2 cups peanut butter
      6 cups Rice Krispies
     12 oz. chocolate chips
     12 oz. butterscotch chips

Bring sugar and Karo to a boil. Add peanut butter and Rice Krispies. Put on a buttered cookie sheet. Melt chocolate and butterscotch chips over hot water and spread over dough. Makes 24 pieces.
—Anna Bender, Middlefield OH

Pink Apple Dessert

      1 cup crushed pineapple
      1 cup pineapple juice plus water
      1 pkg. strawberry Jell-O
      2 large apples, chopped
    1/2 cup chopped nuts
    1-1/2 cups whipped cream
      1 box cottage cheese

Drain crushed pineapple. Heat juice and water to boiling. Dissolve Jell-O in this and cool until partly set. Fold in apples, pineapple and nuts. Fold in whipped cream and add cottage cheese. Pour in dish or mold. Chill until set. *—Mary Beach Baltic OH*

Bill Hentosh

Barbara's Sweet Cinnamon Rolls

  2 cups milk
  2 tablespoons sugar
  2 sticks oleo
4-1/2 teaspoons salt
  2 cups warm water
  5 to 6 cups sugar
  5 pkgs. yeast
  6 eggs, beaten
 11 to 12 cups flour
Butter
Brown sugar
Cinnamon

Heat oleo, milk, sugar and salt until oleo melts. Cool. Mix together warm water, sugar and yeast and let rise. Add eggs and mix all together after the first liquid has cooled (or it will kill the yeast mixture). Add flour and let rise until double. Roll out about 1/2 inch thick on floured top. Sprinkle with brown sugar, cinnamon and pats of butter. Then roll up, cut in 1/2-inch slices and place in greased pie tins. Let rise. Bake in oven at about 375° until toothpick comes out clean. Makes 9 to 10 pie tins. Frost with your favorite frosting.

—Barbara Wagler, Grabill IN

Fruit-Filled Coffee Cake

  4 eggs
  1 cup sugar
  1 cup oil
  2 cups flour
  1 teaspoon baking powder
1/2 teaspoon salt
  6 cups fruit pie filling

Mix first three ingredients. Add dry ingredients. Spread a thin layer of dough into bottom of a 9 x 12 cake pan. Pour filling over batter, then pour rest of batter over filling. Sprinkle with sugar. Bake at 375° until top is nicely browned. Eat hot or cold with milk or ice cream. Black raspberries are a favorite, but we also make with blueberries and blackberries.

—Polly Anna Stoll, Aylmer ON

Texas Special

  1 cup flour
1/2 cup chopped nuts
1/2 cup margarine
  8 oz. soft cream cheese

1 cup powdered sugar
1 cup Cool Whip
1 box instant *or* cooked pudding mix
Chopped nuts

First layer: Mix flour, nuts and margarine until crumbs and press into an 8 x 10 baking dish. Bake 15 minutes at 350°. Second layer: Mix cream cheese, powdered sugar and Cool Whip together. Spread on cooled crust. Add pudding mix and top with Cool Whip or whipped cream and sprinkle with chopped nuts. Refrigerate overnight.

—*Emma Stutzman, Independence IA*

Oatmeal Crisp

2 cups white sugar
2 cups brown sugar
2 cups lard
2 eggs, beaten
1 teaspoon vanilla
1 teaspoon soda
3 cups flour
2 teaspoons oatmeal
1 cup chocolate chips
Nuts and raisins (if desired)

Mix sugar and lard well. Add eggs with vanilla and salt. Blend in flour and baking soda. Add oats. Bake at 400° for 5 to 8 minutes. Makes about 7 dozen cookies.—*Mattie, Lizzie and Mary Wickey Bennington IN*

Easy Chocolate Cake

2 cups sugar
1/2 cup lard
2 eggs
1/2 cup buttermilk
2 cups sifted pastry flour (heaping)
2 tablespoons cocoa (rounded)
1/4 teaspoon baking powder
1/4 teaspoon salt
2 teaspoons baking soda
1 cup boiling water
2 teaspoons vanilla
2 tablespoons salad dressing

Blend all dry ingredients together (except baking soda). Add eggs, shortening, buttermilk and vanilla. Mix boiling water and baking soda (stir well) with other ingredients. Add salad dressing last. Mix well (300 strokes). Bake in 425° oven.

—*Lydia Slabaugh, Viroqua WI*

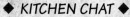

Dairy Queen Ice Cream

    2 envelopes clear gelatin
  1/2 cup cold water
    4 cups milk
    2 cups sugar
    2 teaspoons vanilla
    1 teaspoon salt
    3 cups cream

Mix gelatin with water. Heat milk until hot but not boiling. Remove from heat. Add gelatin, sugar, vanilla and salt. Cool and add cream. Put in refrigerator to chill for 5 or 6 hours before freezing. Makes one gallon. —Lydia Ann Mast
Gladwin MI

Raspberry Angel Food Cake

    2 cups egg whites
  1/2 teaspoon almond extract
    2 teaspoons cream of tartar
    1 teaspoon vanilla
  1/2 teaspoon salt
2-1/4 cups sugar, divided
1-1/2 cups flour
    2 teaspoons raspberry Jell-O powder
      (rounded)

Beat together egg whites, almond extract, cream of tartar, vanilla and salt. Add 1-1/4 cups sugar 2 tablespoons at a time and beat until stiff. Sift together flour and 1 cup sugar and fold in. Add raspberry Jell-O powder and mix in slightly. Place in a tube pan and bake at 325° for 50 to 60 minutes. —Millie Yoder, Oconto WI

Black Magic Cake

    2 cups flour
    2 cups sugar
  3/4 cup cocoa
    2 teaspoons baking soda
    1 teaspoon baking powder
    1 teaspoon salt
    2 eggs
    1 cup strong black coffee
    1 cup boiling water
    1 cup butter
    1 cup milk or sour milk
  1/2 cup vegetable oil
    1 teaspoon vanilla

Combine flour, sugar, cocoa, baking powder, baking soda and salt. Add eggs, coffee, boiling water, butter, milk, oil and vanilla. Beat at medium speed for 2 minutes (batter will be thin). Pour batter into greased pan and bake at 350° for 35 minutes. —Enos Schwartz, Hamilton IN

Cream Caramel Cake

    2 cups brown sugar
    1 pint thick sour cream
    2 eggs, beaten
    2 teaspoons baking soda (dissolved in
      5 tablespoons warm water)
2-1/2 cups flour
    3 teaspoons cocoa
2-1/2 teaspoons baking powder
Vanilla

Mix brown sugar, sour cream and a little vanilla. Add eggs and baking soda. Combine and add flour, cocoa and baking powder. Bake at 350° for 30 to 45 minutes or until done.

Icing

  1/2 cup white sugar
  1/2 cup brown sugar
  1/2 cup cream

Boil together to soft ball stage. Stir until cool. If not thick enough, add a little powder sugar. —Mattie Schwartz, Bloomfield IA

John L. Randolph

Amish Cake

        1/2 cup butter
        1/2 cup boiling water
          1 cup white sugar
          1 cup brown sugar
          2 eggs, beaten
          1 teaspoon baking soda
          1 cup quick oats
      1-1/2 cups flour
          1 teaspoon baking powder
          1 teaspoon vanilla
Pinch of salt

Mix boiling water, butter and sugars until butter melts. Add eggs, baking soda and oats. Sift together flour and baking powder and mix with above followed by vanilla and salt. Bake at 350° for 30 to 40 minutes or 325° for a glass dish.

Topping

          1 cup coconut
          1 cup brown sugar
        1/4 cup milk
          4 tablespoons butter

Boil for 2 minutes and put on cake while still hot. Put in oven to brown crust.
—*Anna Yoder*
Baltic OH

◆ KITCHEN CHAT ◆

THIS MORNING finds us in the kitchen ready to tackle the grapes. Daughter Sara Jane washes the jars with the breakfast dishes while I wash the grapes and put them on the stove to cook. Next we put them through a strainer and let them drip awhile while we get another batch ready to cook.

In the middle of doing the jelly, I stir up some coffee bread using an old recipe from Jake's mom. It needs to rise, so I cover it and leave it for a few hours.

Meantime, my friend Nancy Miller comes calling. She tells me to try making grape butter instead of jelly—it takes only half the time. That sounds like a good idea to me, as I've decided making jelly is a big mess!

Daughter Sara Jane fixes us each a salad for lunch, and we decide what cookies to bake this afternoon. She likes to bake oatmeal cookies like my mother used to make, which are a favorite with the men.

—*Linda Weaver, Middlefield, Ohio*

Peach Crunch

          1 quart peaches
          1 tablespoon sugar
          1 tablespoon flour
        1/2 cup peach juice *or* water
          2 cups sugar
          2 cups flour
        1/2 teaspoon salt
          4 tablespoons butter *or* oleo
          2 eggs, beaten
          4 teaspoons baking powder

Place peaches in baking dish. Mix 1 tablespoon sugar, 1 tablespoon flour and juice and pour over peaches. Combine sugar, flour, baking powder, salt and butter. Add eggs. Sprinkle over peaches. Bake at 400° until brown.
—*Sarah Borntreger*
Mossley ON

Delicious Dessert

Crust

          1 cup flour
        1/2 cup nuts
        1/2 cup oleo

Cut oleo into flour and add nuts. Press into a 9 x 13 pan and bake for 20 minutes at 350°. Cool.

Pudding Mixture

          1 box chocolate pudding
          1 box vanilla pudding
          3 cups milk

Cook and cool, or use instant.

Cheese Mixture

          1 8 oz. cream cheese
          1 cup Cool Whip
          1 cup powdered sugar

Mix cream cheese and powdered sugar. Fold in Cool Whip and spread this mixture on cooled crust. Next spread pudding on cheese mixture. Top with remaining Cool Whip. Sprinkle with chopped nuts. This is also good with butterscotch.
—*Emma Troyer, Williamsfield OH*

Carrot Cake

          2 cups sugar
      1-1/2 cups cooking oil

4 eggs
2 cups flour
2 teaspoons baking powder
2 teaspoons baking soda
2 teaspoons cinnamon
2 teaspoons salt
1/2 cup nuts
3 cups carrots

Sift together flour, baking powder, baking soda, cinnamon and salt. Cream together sugar, eggs and oil. Fold in carrots and nuts.

Frosting

1/2 cup margarine
8 oz. cream cheese
4 cups powdered sugar
1/2 teaspoon butter flavoring
1 teaspoon vanilla

Cream margarine with cream cheese. Add powdered sugar and flavoring.   —*Miriam Bontrager*
Wolcottville IN

Bill Hentosh

Cookies

Sunny Graham Chewies

- 1-2/3 cups graham cracker crumbs
- 2 tablespoons flour
- 1/2 cup butter *or* oleo
- 1-1/2 cups packed brown sugar
- 1/2 cup nuts
- 1/4 teaspoon baking powder
- 2 eggs
- 1 teaspoon vanilla

Combine 1-1/3 cups crumbs, flour and butter in a bowl. Blend until particles form like rice. Pack into greased 9-inch square cake pan. Bake 20 minutes at 350°. Combine sugar, remaining crumbs, nuts, salt and baking powder. Blend. Add beaten eggs and vanilla with brown sugar mixture. Blend well. When crust has baked, pour brown sugar mixture onto the crust. Return to oven and bake 20 minutes more. Cool and cut into squares. —Maria Byler
Quaker City OH

Two Hundred and Fifty Dollar Cookies

- 2 cups butter *or* oleo
- 2 cups white sugar
- 2 cups brown sugar
- 4 eggs, beaten

Pinch of salt
- 2 teaspoons baking powder
- 2 teaspoons baking soda in vinegar
- 2 teaspoons vanilla
- 4 cups flour
- 5 cups oatmeal, blended
- 24 oz. chocolate chips
- 1 8-oz. Hershey bar, grated
- 2 cups finely chopped nuts

Mix the above in order given. Form into balls and place on cookie sheet. Bake 10 minutes at 375°. Makes 112 cookies. —Looina Byler
New Wilmington PA

Jelly-Filled Cookies

- 2 eggs
- 1 cup shortening
- 1-1/2 cups sugar
- 1-1/2 teaspoons baking soda
- 1-1/2 teaspoons cream of tartar
- 4-1/4 cups flour
- 1/2 teaspoon almond extract
- 1/2 teaspoon salt
- 2 teaspoons vanilla

Combine all ingredients. Roll into small balls approximately walnut size. Place on ungreased cookie sheet. Make a thumbprint in the center of each one (do not flatten). Fill thumbprint with 1/4 teaspoon jelly of your choice. Bake at medium heat until very light brown. Frost with a white icing leaving jelly center uncovered. —Lydia Helmuth
Derby IA

◆ KITCHEN CHAT ◆

FOLLOWING our breakfast of orange juice, bacon, cereal and coffee, I packed a lunch for my husband, Menno, who walks to his job at a harness and tack shop.

Daughter Katie and I made up a batch of date-filled cookies, but we "cheated" and stirred the dates into the dough instead of making separate date filling. They turned out nice and are very tasty.

Supper was potatoes, gravy, pork steak and cottage cheese.

—Barbara Troyer, New Wilmington, Pennsylvania

Sugarless Fruit Cookie Recipe

- 1 cup apple juice
- 3/4 cup chopped dates
- 1 small apple, chopped
- 1/2 cup raisins
- 1 cup plus 1 teaspoon flour
- 1 teaspoon cinnamon
- 1 teaspoon baking soda
- 2 teaspoons vanilla
- 2 eggs, beaten

In a large saucepan, combine dates, apples, raisins and juice. Bring to a boil; reduce heat and simmer for 3 minutes. Remove from the heat; cool. Combine flour, cinnamon, baking soda and salt if desired. Stir into apple mixture and mix well. Combine eggs and vanilla; add to batter. Drop by tablespoonfuls onto a nonstick baking sheet. Bake at 350° 10 to 12 minutes. —Helen Beechy
Jamesport MO

Sorghum Cookies

- 4 cups sorghum molasses
- 4 cups white *or* brown sugar
- 3 cups shortening
- 4 eggs
- 1 cup milk
- 2 teaspoons salt
- 2 teaspoons baking powder
- 5 teaspoons ginger
- 8 teaspoons baking soda
- 2 teaspoons vanilla
- 2 teaspoons lemon extract
- 18 cups flour (makes stiff dough)

Form into balls no larger than walnut. Do not flatten. Bake at 350°. Cookies will come off sheets better if allowed to set for about a minute or so.
—*Mattie Borntreger, Cashton WI*

Coffee Cookies

- 4 cups brown sugar
- 2 cups lard
- 2 cups coffee (just like you drink)
- 4 eggs
- 2 teaspoons vanilla
- 2 teaspoons soda
- 6 teaspoons baking powder
- 7 to 8 cups flour

Stir all together and drop by teaspoon. Bake at 350°. Frost with your favorite frosting while cookies are warm.
—*Miriam Bontrager*
Wolcottville IN

◆ KITCHEN CHAT ◆

AT 5 a.m. I lit the gas lamp and started a fire in the Pioneer Maid wood cookstove.

Then I headed for the chicken house with a pail of water for our 15 laying hens, which still lay from 8 to 11 eggs a day. I tell them, "10 eggs a day will keep the ax away!"
—*Joe Borntreger, Cashton, Wisconsin*

Amish Sweet Milk Cookies

- 2 cups brown sugar
- 1 cup white sugar
- 6 eggs, well beaten
- 1-1/4 cups lard
- 2 cups milk
- 5 teaspoons baking powder
- 2 teaspoons baking soda
- 1 teaspoon vanilla *or* nutmeg
- 7 cups flour

Drop with teaspoon.
—*Louella Borntrager*
Sugar Creek OH

Soft Chocolate Chip Cookies

- 3 cups oleo
- 1-1/2 cups white sugar
- 3 cups brown sugar
- 6 eggs

1 12-oz. pkg. chocolate chips
6 tablespoons water
3 teaspoons baking soda
1 teaspoon vanilla
1 teaspoon salt
8 cups flour

Cream oleo and sugar. Add chocolate chips, eggs and water, beating good after each addition. Add baking soda, vanilla, salt and flour. Roll and cut. Bake in hot oven.—*Fannie Byler, Sugar Grove PA*

Mary Ann Raber White Cookies

4 cups brown sugar
4 cups white sugar
4 cups butter *or* lard
4 teaspoons vanilla (in vinegar)
12 teaspoons baking powder
8 eggs
Salt
8 teaspoons baking soda, dissolved
4 cups milk
18 cups flour

Brown 1/2 cup of butter. Keep 1/2 cup from the 4 cups you are supposed to use. Add just before flour. Put a little vinegar in a measuring cup and put your vanilla and baking soda in there. Makes a lot of cookies.　　　*—Barbara Byler, Fredonia PA*

Whoopie Pies (Cookies)

1 cup flour
1 cup cocoa
2 cups sugar
2 teaspoons baking soda
1/2 teaspoon salt
1 cup shortening
2 eggs
2 teaspoons vanilla
1 cup thick sour cream
1 cup cold water

Cream together sugar, salt, eggs, shortening and vanilla. Sift together flour, baking soda and cocoa. Add this to first mixture alternately with water and sour cream. Add a little more flour if not thick enough. Drop by teaspoon and bake in hot oven.

Filling

2 egg whites, beaten
2 cups powdered sugar
1/4 cup soft shortening

1 teaspoon vanilla
4 tablespoons marshmallow cream
1/4 teaspoon salt

Mix until smooth and creamy. Spread between 2 cookies after they are cool.
　　　—*Mattie Gingerich, Edgewood IA*

Amish Filled Cookies

Filling

1 lb. raisins *or* dates
2 cups sugar
2 cups water
4 tablespoons flour

Dough

2 cups sugar
1 cup shortening
2 eggs, beaten
1 cup milk
4 teaspoons baking powder
2 teaspoons baking soda
6-1/2 to 7 cups flour
1/2 teaspoon salt

To make filling: Grind raisins or dates. Add sugar, water and flour. Cook until thick. Chill. To make dough: Cream sugar and shortening. Add eggs, milk, baking powder, baking soda, salt and enough flour to make a soft dough. Chill. Roll thin and cut cookies. Put filling between 2 cookies. Bake at 375° until brown.　　　—*Ella Detweiler, Atlantic PA*

Kootenai Cowboy Cookies

2-1/4 cups shortening
2-1/2 cups brown sugar
2-1/4 cups white sugar
2-1/2 teaspoons vanilla
1/4 teaspoon salt
5 eggs
2-1/2 teaspoons baking soda
1-1/8 teaspoons baking powder
4-1/2 cups flour
4-1/2 cups quick oats
2 cups chocolate chips
1 cup coconut
1 cup nuts

Cream shortening and sugars. Add eggs and vanilla. Stir in dry ingredients in order given. Bake at 375° for 10 minutes. —*Esther Yutzy, Rexford MT*

Chocolate Chip Cookies

1/2 lb. margarine, melted
3/4 cup white sugar
3/4 cup brown sugar
2 eggs
1/2 teaspoon vanilla
1/2 teaspoon maple flavor
1 teaspoon baking soda
1 teaspoon salt
2-1/2 cups flour
1/2 cup chocolate chips
1/2 cup nuts

When margarine has cooled to just warm, stir in the sugar, eggs, flavoring and the rest of the ingredients. Bake in a 400° oven.
—*Katie Schlaback, Loganville WI*

> ◆ KITCHEN CHAT ◆
>
> MOM stirred up a big batch of ginger cookies, but by mistake, she put in nutmeg instead of ginger. They had a rather different taste, but were surprisingly good! Clara rolled them out and baked them.
>
> We washed, peeled and sliced an 8 quarts of apples and then put them on the dryer to dry. Later they'll be used for making delicious pies. Next we washed jars and canned 20 quarts of fresh cider.
>
> —Barbara J.M. Byler, Fredonia, Pennsylvania

> ◆ KITCHEN CHAT ◆
>
> WHILE I was making the bed this morning, I looked out the window just in time to see a big fat opossum going across the creek bank. It probably got so fat on our sweet corn this summer while we had to do with less!
>
> —Mrs. Eli Miller, Apple Creek, Ohio

Amish Sugar Cookies

1 cup sugar
1 cup cooking oil
2 eggs
1 teaspoon cream of tartar
1 teaspoon vanilla
1 cup powdered sugar
1 cup margarine
4-1/2 cups flour
1 teaspoon baking soda

Combine sugars, margarine and oil and beat well. Add eggs, beat again and add remaining ingredients. Drop on cookie sheets and flatten with fork. Bake in moderate oven until light brown.
—*Susan Byler, Spartansburg PA*

Doyle Yoder

Ronald N. Wilson

Bill Hentosh

Chewy Oatmeal Cookies

    4 cups flour, sifted
    3 teaspoons baking soda
    2 teaspoons salt
    4 teaspoons cinnamon
    1 teaspoon nutmeg
    3 cups shortening *or* margarine
5-1/3 cups packed brown sugar
    8 eggs
    8 cups oats
    4 cups raisins
Vanilla

Sift flour, baking soda, salt and spices into bowl. Add shortening, sugar, eggs and vanilla. Beat until smooth. Stir in oats and raisins.

—Amanda Gingerich, Smiths Grove KY

Amish Church Cookies

    2 cups brown sugar
    1 cup granulated sugar
    3 eggs, beaten
1-1/2 cups shortening
1-1/2 cups milk
    2 teaspoons baking soda
    2 teaspoons baking powder
    2 teaspoons vanilla
    1 teaspoon lemon extract
6-3/4 cups flour

Cream eggs, sugar and shortening together. Beat in vanilla and lemon. Add dry ingredients and milk. Drop by spoonful on cookie sheet. Bake at 400°. Makes 6 dozen.   *—Katie Hochstetler, Topeka IN*

Peanut Butter Bars

1/2 cup white sugar
1/2 cup brown sugar
1/2 cup butter *or* oleo
  1 egg, beaten
1/4 teaspoon salt
1/2 teaspoon baking soda
1/2 teaspoon vanilla
  1 cup peanut butter
  1 cup flour
  1 cup quick oats

Cream sugar and butter. Add egg and all other ingredients. Pour batter in greased 7 x 11 baking dish. Bake at 350° for 25 minutes.

Icing

  1 cup semisweet chocolate morsels
1/2 cup powdered sugar
1/4 cup peanut butter
  2 to 4 tablespoons milk

Arrange chocolate morsels over top as soon as you remove from oven. Spread to cover the edges. Spread mixture of powdered sugar, peanut butter and milk over the top of the chocolate and swirl slightly. Cut in bars while slightly warm.

—Edna Mae Miller, Dundee OH

Nate Schwarz

Grandma Miller's Sugar Cookies

    4 eggs
    4 cups sugar
    1 cup shortening, melted
    2 cups milk
    3 teaspoons baking soda
    3 teaspoons baking powder
Flour

Use just enough flour so the dough handles well. Sprinkle the cookies with sugar before baking. Bake in hot oven.

—Susan Byler
Spartansburg PA

Chocolate Chip Blonde Brownies

    2/3 cup butter, softened
      2 tablespoons hot water
1-1/2 cups brown sugar
      2 eggs
      2 teaspoons vanilla
      2 cups flour
      1 teaspoon baking powder
    1/4 teaspoon baking soda
      1 teaspoon salt
    1/2 cup chocolate chips

Cream butter and sugar. Add hot water, eggs and vanilla. Beat well. Add dry ingredients. Spread in greased 9 x 13 pan. Sprinkle chocolate chips over the top. Bake at 350° for 25 to 30 minutes. Cool slightly and cut in squares. —Linda Millers Windsor MO

Chocolate Chip Bars

      1 cup butter *or* oleo
    1/2 cup white sugar
    1/2 cup brown sugar
      3 egg yolks
      1 tablespoon water
      2 cups flour
    1/4 teaspoon baking soda
      1 teaspoon baking powder
      1 teaspoon vanilla
    1/2 cup nuts

Meringue

      3 egg whites, beaten stiff
    3/4 cup brown sugar
    1/2 teaspoon vanilla

Cream together sugars and butter. Add egg yolks and water and beat well. Add flour, baking soda, baking powder and vanilla and mix well. Spread on large greased cookie sheet. Sprinkle chocolate chips and nuts gently over batter and press down. Mix meringue ingredients together and spread over cookie dough. Bake at 350° for 25 minutes.
—Ann Miller, Mio MI

Old-Fashioned Oat Nut Cookies

      3 cups quick oats
      3 cups flour
      1 cup brown sugar
      1 cup white sugar
      1 cup butter and lard (1/2 of each,
melted)
      1 cup raisins
      1 cup boiling water
      1 cup nut meats
      1 cup shredded coconut
      2 eggs, beaten
      1 teaspoon baking powder
      1 teaspoon baking soda
      2 teaspoons cinnamon
      1 teaspoon nutmeg
    1/2 teaspoon cloves
  1-1/2 teaspoons vanilla
  1-1/2 teaspoons salt

Mix the dry ingredients in a large bowl. Make a hole in the center and add the melted butter and lard, eggs, vanilla and water. Stir until mixed, then drop by teaspoonful on a cookie sheet. Bake in moderate to hot oven until golden brown. Makes 5-1/2 dozen. —Lovina Miller, Canton MN

◆ KITCHEN CHAT ◆

OLDEST daughter Marilyn got the peppers in from the garden, which is pretty empty now. She cut them and put them through the Salad Master to use later for salads, pizza, casseroles and such—got about 15 cups.

Meanwhile, I mixed together a big batch of chocolate chip cookies and baked them.

The men came in for lunch at 11:30. We had soup, lettuce sandwiches, cookies and apples. Afterward, Marilyn took the peppers to the neighbors' to keep in their freezer.
—Mrs. Paul Miller, Millersburg, Ohio

Chocolate Chip Cookies

      4 cups butter *or* margarine
      4 cups brown sugar
      4 cups white sugar
      8 eggs
      8 teaspoons vanilla
      4 teaspoons baking soda
      4 teaspoons salt
    12 cups flour
      4 cups nuts
Chocolate chips as preferred

Mix and drop by teaspoon onto a greased cookie sheet. Bake at 400° until light brown.
—Sylvia Stutzman, Columbia KY

Chocolate Chip Cookies

    2 cups brown sugar
    2 cups white sugar
    2 teaspoons salt
    2 cups shortening
    1 teaspoon vanilla
    4 teaspoons baking soda
    6 eggs
    4 teaspoons cream of tartar
    7 cups flour
    2 or 3 pkgs. chocolate chips

Mix well in order given. Drop by teaspoonful on cookie sheet and bake at 375° to 400°.

—Viola Mast, Blanchard MI

Sugar Cookies

        3 cups brown sugar
    1-1/2 cups soft butter
        3 eggs
        1 cup milk
        1 teaspoon vanilla
        2 teaspoons baking soda
        4 teaspoons baking powder
        5 cups flour

Mix sugar and butter. Add eggs and mix well. Add rest of the ingredients. Drop by teaspoonful onto a cookie sheet. Bake at 350° until light brown. Don't overbake. Frost them with caramel frosting while the cookies are still warm. *—Elsie Yoder Sugar Creek OH*

Butterscotch Crunch Cookies

    2 cups lard

    2 cups brown sugar
    2 cups white sugar
    5 cups flour
    6 cups oats
    3 teaspoons vanilla
    3 teaspoons maple flavor
    2 teaspoons salt
    2 teaspoons baking soda
    4 eggs, beaten

Mix together dry ingredients. Add lard, then eggs with flavoring. Make into rolls and let set overnight. Cut and bake until golden brown.

—Fannie A. Hershberger, Dalton OH

Ronald N. Wilson

Snitz (Dried Apple) Cookies

    1 cup shortening
    2 cups brown sugar
    2 eggs, beaten
    1 cup snitz, cooked
    1/2 cup raisins
    4 cups flour
    2 teaspoons baking powder
    2 teaspoons baking soda
    1/2 teaspoon salt
    1 teaspoon cinnamon

Cream together sugar and shortening. Add eggs, snitz and raisins. Sift together dry ingredients and add alternately to the above. Drop on cookie sheet and bake at 350°. I let dough stand overnight.
—Mrs. Dan Yoder, Baltic OH

◆ KITCHEN CHAT ◆

I STARTED a fire under the kettle to heat up the wash water, then made our breakfast of tomato gravy, sausage and cereal. Amos went out and hitched up "Jake" and "Dollie" to rake hay.

Dinner was potatoes, corn, pork, applesauce, fruit and cake. This afternoon some neighbors were here to help fill the silo, so after I got the children settled down for a nap I baked three apple pies and fixed bologna sandwiches to feed them. When I went out, two of the men had already left, so the rest had plenty!

We had a late supper of banana soup, fresh tomatoes and popcorn.

—Viola Mast, Blanchard, Michigan

Monster Cookies

    12 eggs
    4 cups brown sugar
    4 cups white sugar
    1 tablespoon vanilla
    1 tablespoon Karo
    8 teaspoons baking soda
    1 lb. butter or oleo
    3 lbs. peanut butter
    18 cups oats
    1 lb. chocolate chips
    1 lb. M&M candy

Mix in order given. Drop by spoonful on greased cookie sheet. Bake at 350° about 12 to 15 minutes. Do not overbake.   —Anna Yoder, Baltic OH

Cut-Out Cream Cookies

    2 cups granulated sugar
    2 eggs
    1 cup oleo
    1 cup sour cream
    1 teaspoon baking soda
    1/2 teaspoon salt
    1 teaspoon lemon extract
    5 cups flour

Mix together all ingredients except flour. Fold in flour; dough will be soft. Chill for a few hours. Roll out 1/4 inch thick on floured board. Cut in desired shapes and sprinkle with sugar or frost. Bake at 325° for 10 to 12 minutes.   —Linda Yoder
Quaker OH

Coffee Bars

    2-2/3 cups brown sugar
    1 cup cooking oil
    1 cup warm coffee
    1 teaspoon baking soda
    1 teaspoon salt
    1 teaspoon vanilla
    2 eggs, beaten
    3 cups flour

Mix all together. Bake at 350° for 20 to 25 minutes. Chocolate chips can be sprinkled on top before baking if desired, or ice with the following:

Chocolate Peanut Butter Icing

    1/2 stick oleo or butter
    2 tablespoons cocoa
    3 tablespoons milk
    1 tablespoon peanut butter
    1/2 lb. powdered sugar
    1 teaspoon vanilla

Bring oleo, cocoa, milk and peanut butter to a boil. Add powdered sugar and vanilla. Spread on bars and cut in squares.

Homemade Icing

    1 cup white sugar
    2 cups milk
    4 teaspoons cornstarch

Boil 5 to 7 minutes.   —Emma Miller, Orrville OH

Fannie Schwartz

Condiments

Fruit Slush

- 1 12-oz. can orange juice, fixed as directed
- 8 bananas, sliced or chopped
- 1 cup crushed pineapple
- 1 cup hot water
- 1 cup white sugar

Dissolve sugar in hot water. Add rest of ingredients and freeze. Stir several times while freezing. Remove from freezer one hour before serving.

—*Ruby Beach, Sugar Creek OH*

Homemade Catsup

- 2-1/2 gals. tomato juice
- 1/2 cup salt
- 2 medium onions, shredded
- 1 teaspoon cinnamon
- 1 teaspoon cloves
- 2-1/2 cups vinegar
- 8 cups sugar
- 1/2 cup flour

Boil down 1/3 of tomato juice and add salt, onions cinnamon, cloves and vinegar. Mix well. Add sugar and flour to juice. Keep stirring it well while adding ingredients so it will stay smooth. Bring to a boil and fill jars. Consult a canning guide for processing directions.

—*Rebecca Schrock, Milan MO*

Ronald N. Wilson

◆ KITCHEN CHAT ◆

AT 3:20 the boys came home from school. I put them to work carrying wood into the kitchen for the cookstove and carrying 58 quarts of applesauce, which daughter Savilla and I canned earlier, to the basement.

Then it was high time to think about getting supper, which consisted of scalloped potatoes, canned beef, baked beans, cole slaw and canned peaches for dessert.

—*Ella Detweiler, Atlantic, Pennsylvania*

Nate Schwartz

Hamburger Pickles

- 1 gal. pickles, thinly sliced
- 1 gal. water
- 1 cup salt
- 1 tablespoon alum (heaping)

Syrup

- 3 lbs. sugar
- 1 pt. vinegar
- 1 pt. water
- 1 tablespoon whole allspice
- 1 tablespoon celery seed

Put pickles in salt brine of water and salt for 3 days. Drain off and wash in clear water. Boil pickles in water and alum to cover for 10 minutes. Make syrup of sugar, vinegar and water. Put allspice and celery seed in a small bag and add to syrup. Cook until clear and glossy. Consult a canning guide for processing directions.

—Mary Miller, Punxsutawney PA

For Pickles

- 2 cups sugar
- 2 cups vinegar

Onions

- 1 tablespoon celery seed
- 1 tablespoon garlic
- 1 tablespoon pepper

Mix above ingredients and add enough water to fill a gallon jar. Keep in a cool place for 2 weeks. Shake slightly daily. Then ready to eat.

—Edna Miller, Clark MO

V-8 Juice

- 1/2 bushel tomatoes, chopped
- 1 bunch of celery
- 4 onions, chopped
- 2 green peppers, chopped
- 8 whole cloves (added to tomatoes before cooking)
- 1/2 cup sugar
- 1/4 cup salt

Juice of 3 lemons

Cook vegetables until soft. Put through a sieve. Return to kettle. Add sugar, salt and lemon juice. Consult a canning guide for processing directions. —Mrs. Amos Eicher, Oconto WI

> ### ◆ KITCHEN CHAT ◆
> I COOKED a big batch of applesauce from our own Courtland apples that my husband, Abe, picked. We prefer Courtlands over any tart early varieties—they take a lot less sugar and have a rosy taste when cooked.
>
> For supper we had mock turkey casserole, fried potato cakes, corn, applesauce and oreo pudding. Son Daniel, 17, didn't get to eat with the rest of the family because he had to work late at the sale barn unloading a truckload of hay. When he got home, he acted like he was about starved!
>
> —Esther Troyer, Sugarcreek, Ohio

MAUDIE and Andy Raber raised eight children (seven girls and one boy) on their 80-acre farm in the hills of Holmes County, Ohio.

Andy tends heifers and sheep and also runs a sawmill with help from their son. Maudie plants a large garden each year.

When time allows, Maudie and her daughters serve Amish-style meals (by reservation only) to tour groups in their home. Dinners are a family affair with everyone involved, including Andy, who serves as "water boy", filling glasses and conversing with the guests.

If you'd like to join a tour group for a meal in Maudie's kitchen (along with several other fascinating stops in Amish country), write World Wide Country Tours, Dept. AKB, 5925 Country Lane, Greendale WI 53129 and request the Amish Country brochure.

Recipes in this chapter are from Maudie's own cookbook, *Raber's Country Kitchen*. To order a copy, send $5.95 (includes shipping) to Maudie Raber, 3497 CR 135, Millersburg OH 44654.

Maudie's Kitchen

Sweet and Sour Salad Dressing

5 cups sugar
1-2/3 cups vinegar
5 cups oil
1-1/2 tablespoons salt
1-1/2 tablespoons celery seed
1-1/4 teaspoons pepper
3/4 cup salad dressing
1/2 cup mustard
1/2 onion

Maudie's Favorite Bread

1/2 cup white sugar
1/4 cup lard
2 tablespoons salt
2 cups hot water
2 cups Robin Hood flour

Mix the above ingredients together. Then beat 2 eggs and add to first ingredients. Soak 2 tablespoons yeast in 3/4 cup lukewarm water and let it set for 7 minutes, then add to first mixture. Add another 2 cups of flour and let it set for 20 minutes, then stir real well and work in the rest of the flour, only enough to handle. (If it's too stiff, it makes dry, hard bread.) Let rise till double in bulk, knead down, let rise again. Then work out in pans and let rise until you have nice round loaves. Bake at 350° for 20 minutes. Makes 4 small or 3 large loaves.

Three Bean Salad

5 qts. yellow wax beans
5 qts. green string beans
1 qt. small onions
2 qts. red kidney beans (drained)—do not cook
1 lg. bunch of celery
12 large carrots
2 heads cauliflower

Cut up vegetables into 1-inch pieces and cook until tender. Salt to taste. Cook vegetables separately. Drain all vegetables and discard juice except onion and celery water. Make a syrup with the following ingredients:

10 cups vinegar
5 cups sugar
1-1/2 tablespoons mixed pickle spices
5 sticks cinnamon
10 cups water and juice from celery and onion (2 cups)

Boil until sugar is dissolved. Pack vegetables in sterile jars and pour syrup over vegetables to 1/2 inch of jar top. Consult a canning guide for processing directions.

Buttermilk Donuts

4 cups Robin Hood flour
1 cup sugar
1 cup buttermilk
1 teaspoon salt
1 teaspoon soda
1 teaspoon baking powder
2 eggs, well beaten
3 tablespoons oleo, melted
1 teaspoon vanilla

Cream sugar, butter and eggs. Add salt, soda, baking powder, vanilla and mix well. Add flour and buttermilk, alternating. Roll out dough and cut with donut cutter. Deep fry in oil, turning once. Drain on paper towels. Dip in white sugar or powdered sugar while still hot.

> ### ◆ MAUDIE'S MUSINGS ◆
> WE HAVE eight children—all are boys but seven, and each has a brother. They are all married but the two youngest, Betty and Linda, who help with the cooking. Betty also does our bookkeeping for Andy's sawmill and my cooking business. The rest all live within 5 miles and also help with cooking whenever we need them. Some of our 17 grandchildren are "cooks in training".

Our Favorite Dressing for Tossed Salad

2 cups Miracle Whip
1 cup sugar
1/2 teaspoon onion salt
3/4 teaspoon salt
1 tablespoon mustard
1/2 cup cream

Beat well. This dressing keeps for a long time.

1/2 teaspoon salt
1/4 teaspoon pepper
1 can kidney beans
1 can butter beans
1 can lima beans
1/2 cup catsup
1/2 cup brown sugar
1/8 cup vinegar
3/4 teaspoon dry mustard

Save part of bacon for top. Fry beef, bacon and onion till brown. Drain off fat. Mix all ingredients together. Top with rest of bacon. Bake 1 hour, covered, at 350°.

Mock Ham Loaf

1 lb. hamburger
1/2 lb. wieners (ground)
1 egg, beaten
Salt and pepper
1 cup cracker crumbs

Mix above ingredients.

Sauce

1/2 cup brown sugar
1/4 cup water
1/2 cup tomato juice
1 tablespoon vinegar
1 teaspoon mustard

Mix half of the sauce mixture into meat. Thicken the other half and put on top when half baked. Bake about one hour at 350°.

Luscious Sweet Rolls

1/2 cup lukewarm water
1 tablespoon yeast

Soak the yeast in the water.

1 cup mashed potatoes
2/3 cup shortening
1/2 cup sugar
2 eggs
1 cup lukewarm scalded milk
7 cups Robin Hood flour

Mix in order. Work real well. Let rise till double in size. Roll out 1/2 inch thick. Spread with butter, brown sugar and cinnamon. Roll and cut into 1/2-inch pieces. Let rise until double, approximately 1 hour. Bake at 350° for 15 minutes.

Three Bean Hot Dish

1 lb. ground beef
1/2 lb. bacon, cut up
1 onion

Dutch Apple Pie

9-inch unbaked pie shell

Pour into pie shell:

    3 cups pared, sliced apples

Stir together:

    1 cup sugar
    3 tablespoons flour
    1/2 teaspoon cinnamon

Combine, then mix with the above mixture:

    1 egg, beaten
    1 cup light cream
    1 teaspoon vanilla

Pour over apples. Sprinkle with:

    1/2 cup chopped nuts

Dot with:

    1 tablespoon butter

Bake at 350° for 45 to 50 minutes until apples are tender.

Hot Potato Salad

Fry bacon in pan, leaving about 2 tablespoons of bacon oil. Take bacon out and add 1 can cream of mushroom or celery soup.

    1 tablespoon sugar
    1/3 cup milk
    2 tablespoons vinegar
    1/2 teaspoon salt

Bring to a boil. Add 4 hard-boiled eggs, chopped. Add 4 potatoes, cooked and diced. Simmer until hot.

Erma's Shoo-Fly Pie

    1-1/4 cups brown sugar
    1-1/4 cups dark Karo
    3 eggs, beaten
    3 heaping tablespoons flour
    3 cups cold water

Mix all together then make crumbs with the following ingredients. Put syrup in unbaked pie crust then crumbs on top.

Crumbs

    2 cups flour
    1-1/2 cups brown sugar
    3/4 cup oleo

    1 teaspoon soda
    1 teaspoon cream of tartar
    1 teaspoon cinnamon
    1/4 teaspoon nutmeg
    1/4 teaspoon ginger
    1/2 teaspoon cloves
Salt

Bake at 375° for 25 to 30 minutes. Makes 2 pies.

Ronald N. Wilson

Amish Cake

       1 cup rolled oats
 1-1/2 cups boiling water
   1/2 cup butter *or* oleo
       1 cup white sugar
       1 cup brown sugar
 1-1/2 cups flour
       2 eggs
       1 teaspoon vanilla
       1 teaspoon soda

Add all ingredients and mix well. Bake at 350° for 35 minutes.

Topping

       1 cup brown sugar
   1/2 cup cream
       1 tablespoon butter
Coconut *or* nuts

Boil sugar, cream and butter for 1 minute. Add coconut or nuts. Spread on hot cake. Place under broiler until golden brown.

Turkey or Chicken Supreme

       2 cups cooked, diced meat
       2 cups uncooked macaroni
       2 cups milk
       2 cans cream of chicken soup

1 cup Velveeta cheese
1 medium onion, diced
1/2 teaspoon salt
1/4 teaspoon pepper
3 tablespoons butter, melted

Mix all ingredients together except cheese. Put in a greased casserole and refrigerate overnight. Remove from refrigerator several hours before baking. Bake at 350° for 1-1/2 hours. Top with cheese during the last part of baking.

Vanilla Crumb Pie

Filling

1 cup brown sugar
2 cups water
2 eggs, well beaten
1 cup light Karo
3 tablespoons flour
Touch of vanilla

Boil until thick, then pour hot into a hot baked pie crust. Spread crumbs on top and bake until brown.

Crumbs

Blend together:

1 cup flour
1/4 cup white sugar
1/4 cup lard
1/2 teaspoon soda
1/2 teaspoon cream of tartar

Makes 2 pies.

Mom's Dressing

1 loaf of bread
1 cup cooked and diced potatoes
Plus some broth
1 cup diced celery
2 cups cooked chicken, cut fine

Cut bread in 1-inch squares and toast in butter. Add rest of ingredients. Beat 6 eggs and add:

3 cups milk
1 tablespoon seasoned salt
1 teaspoon salt
Pepper and parsley

Mix all together, then fry in skillet with butter. Can be fried enough to eat right away or fried light and put in roaster. Put in oven for 20 minutes at 300°.

Ground Beef Casserole

1 can oven-ready biscuits (buttermilk)
1-1/2 lbs. hamburger
1/2 cup chopped onion
4 oz. cream cheese
1/4 cup milk
1 can mushroom *or* chicken soup
1 teaspoon salt
1/2 cup catsup

Brown meat and onions. Drain. Mix all together. Bake at 375° for 10 minutes. Place biscuits on top and bake 15-20 minutes. Serves 6. This can be made the day before. Make sure it's hot before you put biscuits on or they get too brown.

Butterscotch Sauce for Angel Food Cake

In a saucepan, combine:

- 3/4 cup sugar
- 1/2 cup light corn syrup
- 1/4 teaspoon salt
- 1/4 cup butter
- 1/2 cup cream

Cook over low heat, stirring constantly until mixture reaches soft ball stage (234°). Stir in:

- 1/2 cup cream

Continue cooking and stirring until thick and smooth. Remove from heat. Stir in:

- 1/2 teaspoon vanilla

Serve on angel food cake.

Peanut Brittle

- 2 cups white sugar
- 1 cup light Karo
- 1/2 cup water
- 2 cups peanuts
- 1 heaping teaspoon soda

Boil sugar, Karo, water and a bit of salt together until it thickens a little. Add peanuts and boil until brittle. Add soda and pour in greased pan. When cool, break.

◆ MAUDIE'S MUSINGS ◆

WE STARTED serving meals to tourists in 1980. As is custom, our girls only went to school through 8th grade, and afterward I felt they needed more work to keep out of mischief before they were old enough to work outside the home.

The first few years we only hosted a couple of groups a month, but as the years passed we did more and more. We never advertised.

Meals are by reservation only, and we ask for 15 or more. The most we served in one day was 120 people (three bus loads) at three different times. The least we had was one man from Japan who was real desperate!

Upside Down Date Pudding

1 cup boiling water
1 cup dates

Pour boiling water over dates. Cool. Mix the following in another bowl:

1/2 cup white sugar
1/2 cup brown sugar
1-1/2 cups flour
1 teaspoon soda
1 teaspoon salt
1 teaspoon baking powder

Add the date mixture and following ingredients.

1 egg
2 tablespoons melted oleo
1 cup nuts

Sauce to pour over top

1-1/2 cups boiling water
1-1/2 cups brown sugar
1 tablespoon oleo

Bake 35 minutes at 350°.

Brown Sugar Dumplings

1 cup brown sugar
3/4 cup milk
2 cups flour
1 tablespoon butter
2 teaspoons baking powder
1 cup nuts, dates *or* raisins (optional)

Pour the following in a cake pan and bring to a boil:

1-1/2 cups brown sugar
1 tablespoon butter
2 cups water

Drop dough batter by spoonful in hot syrup and bake 25 minutes at 325°.

Rocky Road Candy

3 lbs. chocolate
3/4 lb. butter
10 oz. marshmallows
1 lb. nuts

Melt chocolate and cool down to 90°. Put in butter which has been at room temperature. Mixture will get very thick. Then cool again for a length of time till it gets a little hard around edges. Then beat for about 10 minutes. Mix in marshmallows and nuts.

Ronald N. Wilson

Maple Sponge Pudding

Combine, let set 5 minutes:

1 envelope (1 tablespoon) unflavored gelatin
1-1/2 cups cold water

Combine in a saucepan:

2 cups brown sugar
1/2 cup hot water

Bring to a boil and boil 5 minutes. Pour syrup gradually into soaking gelatin; set aside to cool. In a separate saucepan, combine and cook until thickened; cool.

2 cups milk
1 cup sugar
2-1/2 tablespoons flour
1 egg, beaten
Maple flavoring

Blend both mixtures, then fold in:

2 cups whipped cream
Chopped peanuts *or* walnuts
Sliced bananas, optional

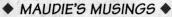

Oven-Baked Caramel Corn

    2   cups brown sugar
    1   teaspoon salt
    1   teaspoon baking soda
    6   quarts popped corn
    1   cup oleo
  1/2   cup light Karo
    1   teaspoon butterscotch flavoring

Boil sugar, butter, syrup and salt together for 5 minutes. Remove from heat and add soda and flavoring. Pour over popped corn and stir well. Spread on cookie sheet and bake one hour at 200°, stirring every 15 minutes. Remove from oven and cool.

Cheese Pie

Crust

   20   graham crackers, rolled fine
  1/4   cup sugar
  1/4   cup oleo *or* butter

Press mixture into pie pan.

Filling

   16   oz. cream cheese
    1   small can crushed pineapple, drained
    2   eggs, beaten
  1/2   teaspoon vanilla

Fold in lightly and sprinkle top with cinnamon. Bake at 375° for 20 minutes.

Sour Cream Coffee Cake

  1/2   cup margarine
    1   cup sugar
    2   eggs

    1   teaspoon baking powder
    1   teaspoon soda
    2   cups flour
    1   cup sour cream
Touch of vanilla

Topping

  1/2   cup chopped nuts
  1/2   cup sugar
  1/2   teaspoon cinnamon

Beat oleo and sugar. Add eggs, vanilla and sour cream. Add dry ingredients. Put half of batter in greased pan, then half of topping. Add rest of batter and topping. Bake at 350° for 40-45 minutes.

Don Shenk

Honey Cookies

- 1 cup butter *or* lard
- 2 cups honey
- 8 cups flour
- 1/2 teaspoon cinnamon
- 1/2 teaspoon allspice
- 2 teaspoons vanilla
- 2 eggs
- 4 teaspoons soda

Boil butter and honey together 1 minute, then cool. Stir in vanilla and eggs. Add soda. Sift flour and spice together. Make in rolls or roll out.

Southern Pecan Bars

Cream:

- 1/3 cup butter *or* margarine, softened
- 1/2 cup brown sugar

Blend in:

- 1-1/3 cups flour
- 1/2 teaspoon baking powder

Stir in:

- 1/4 cup finely chopped pecans

Pat firmly into a well-greased 9" x 13" pan and bake at 350° for 10 minutes. Cover with pecan topping and bake an additional 25-30 minutes. Let cool before cutting into bars. Yields 30 bars.

Pecan Topping

Combine, then pour over partially baked crust:

- 2 eggs, beaten
- 3/4 cup dark corn syrup
- 1/4 cup brown sugar
- 3 tablespoons flour
- 1/2 teaspoon salt
- 1 teaspoon vanilla

Sprinkle with:

- 3/4 cup chopped pecans

Fresh Apple Cake

- 4 cups chopped apples
- 1 cup raisins
- 1 cup nuts
- 2 cups sugar
- 3 cups flour

- 1/4 cup salad oil
- 2 eggs
- 1 teaspoon vanilla
- 1/2 teaspoon nutmeg
- 1/2 teaspoon salt

Dump all together and mix in large mixing bowl. Grease a 9 x 13 inch pan. Bake 1 hour at 325° or a little longer.

Icing

- 1/4 lb. butter
- 1 cup sugar
- 2/3 cup milk

Beat these three ingredients together. Mix:

- 8 tablespoons *or* 1/3 cup shortening
- 3 tablespoons flour, one at a time
- 1 teaspoon vanilla

Beat 12 minutes.

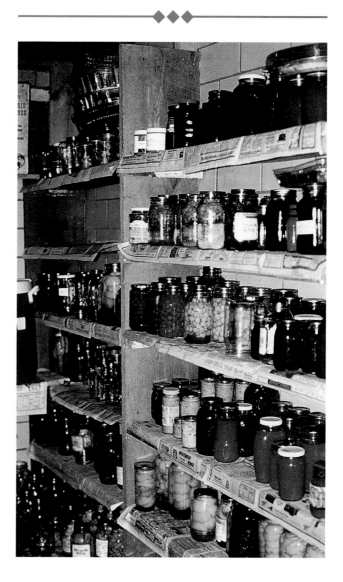

Chili Sauce

- 12 ripe tomatoes
- 1 red pepper
- 1 large onion
- 1 teaspoon salt
- 1 teaspoon allspice
- 1 teaspoon ground nutmeg
- 1 green pepper
- 2 cups vinegar
- 1 teaspoon ground ginger
- 1 cup brown sugar
- 1 teaspoon cinnamon

Remove the skins from tomatoes and chop with the peppers and onions. Add the vinegar, brown sugar and spices and bring to a boil. Stir to prevent burning. Boil for about one hour or until it begins to thicken. Pour the sauce in hot jars. Consult a canning guide for processing directions.

Whoopie Pie Cookies

- 1 cup shortening
- 2 cups sugar
- 2 eggs

Beat together and add:

- 1 cup milk
- 1/2 cup cocoa
- 5 cups flour
- Pinch of salt
- Vanilla

Beat well, then add:

- 1 cup hot water
- 2 teaspoons soda, dissolved in water

Drop by teaspoonful on cookie sheet.

Whoopie Pie Filling

Beat:

- 2 eggs
- 2 teaspoons vanilla
- 2 tablespoons milk
- 4 cups powdered sugar
- 1/2 cup Crisco

Hamburger Pickles

- 1 gal. cucumbers, unpeeled

Slice very thin in a salt brine of 1 cup salt to 1 gal. water. Put in a crock with a cloth and plate over them for 3 to 5 days. Then drain and wash in cold water. Boil 10 minutes in alum water containing:

- 1 tablespoon alum
- Water to cover the cucumbers

Now wash again. You are now ready to put them in the syrup.

- 1 to 2 cups vinegar
- 2 cups water
- 6 cups sugar
- 1 tablespoon whole cloves
- 1 tablespoon allspice
- 1 tablespoon celery seed
- 1 stick cinnamon

Put spice in bag and cook with the pickles to a boil. Cook until they look transparent or clear. Consult a canning guide for processing directions.

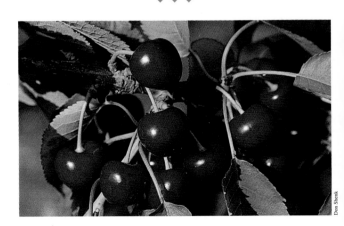

Don Shenk

For Soaking Steaks

- 1 cup soy sauce
- 1 teaspoon ginger
- 1 teaspoon dry mustard
- 1 teaspoon Accent
- 3 to 6 cloves
- 1/2 teaspoon garlic, scant
- 1/2 cup salad oil

Soak overnight.

Pizza Sauce

- 1/2 bushel tomatoes
- 3 lbs. onions
- 4 large hot peppers

Cook this together for 2-1/2 to 3 hours. Strain and add:

- 1-1/2 cups sugar
- 1-1/2 cups oil
- 1/2 cup salt
- 1 tablespoon basil leaves
- 1 tablespoon oregano leaves
- 4 12-oz. cans tomato paste

Cook 1 hour, then freeze in containers.

Cinnamon Pickles

- 2 gal. large cucumbers, peeled, seeded and chunked

Soak in 8-1/2 quarts water and 2 cups lime for 24 hours. Drain and wash. Soak in cold water for 3 hours. Place in large kettle and simmer for 2 hours in the following solution:

- 1 cup vinegar, color to suit
- 1 tablespoon alum

Enough water to cover

Drain off liquid and make a syrup of:

- 3 cups vinegar
- 3 cups water
- 6 sticks cinnamon
- 1 tablespoon salt
- 10 cubes sugar
- 10 oz. red cinnamon candy

Bring to a boil and pour over pickles. Let stand overnight. Drain off liquid and heat this syrup every 24 hours for 3 days. On the fourth day, process. Consult a canning guide for processing directions.

◆ MAUDIE'S MUSINGS ◆

WE DO NOT always have a big breakfast like some Amish families do. If we're expecting guests and I have a busy day of cooking, I have to start baking bread and pies by 4:30 or 5 a.m. The rest of the family gets up about 6, and by that time I have grabbed a bite of something with my coffee, so they just have a bite, too.

The days that we aren't expecting guests, we eat breakfast together, mostly cereal, rolls or cake. As a special treat for Andy, I will fry some corn mush, which he really enjoys.

If we don't have a bus load to cook dinner for, we usually have something different like spaghetti, pizza or soup for our dinner. Sometimes for a special treat we will take a buggy ride to the Burger King in Berlin. Wow!

Buttermilk Cookies

- 2 cups brown sugar
- 1 cup white sugar
- 1 cup butter *or* lard
- 4 eggs
- 1 teaspoon soda
- 1/2 teaspoon cream of tartar
- 1 cup buttermilk
- 5 cups flour

Touch of maple flavoring

Put soda and cream of tartar in buttermilk. Mix the remaining ingredients together and either drop on cookie sheet or press through a cookie press. Bake at 375°.

Ronald N. Wilson

Bishop's Chocolate Pie

Combine until crumbly:

- 2 cups flour
- 1/2 cup brown sugar
- 1/2 cup chopped nuts
- 1 cup margarine, softened

Spread on a cookie sheet and bake at 350° for 15 minutes. Remove from oven, crumble, then pat into a 9" x 13" pan. Cool. Beat together:

- 2 3-1/2-oz. boxes French vanilla instant pudding
- 2 3-1/2-oz. boxes chocolate instant pudding
- 4 cups milk

Blend with:

- 4 cups vanilla ice cream, softened

Pour onto crust; refrigerate until well set. Spread over top:

- 8 oz. frozen whipped topping, thawed

Shave, then sprinkle on pie:

- 1 1-3/4-oz. solid chocolate candy bar

Butterscotch Torte

- 6 eggs, separated
- 1 cup white sugar
- 1 teaspoon baking powder
- 2 teaspoons almond flavoring
- 2 cups graham cracker crumbs
- 1 cup chopped walnuts

Beat egg yolks well. Slowly add sugar, baking powder and almond flavoring. Beat egg whites until stiff. Add to yolk mixture. Fold in crumbs and walnuts. Bake at 350° for 30 to 35 minutes.

Sauce

- 1/4 cup butter
- 1/4 cup water
- 1 cup brown sugar
- 1 tablespoon flour
- 1 egg, beaten
- 1/4 cup orange juice
- 1 teaspoon vanilla

Melt butter in saucepan. Add water. Blend in brown sugar, flour, egg, orange juice and vanilla. Cook until thickened. Pour over cake when cooled. First put whipped cream over cake, then sauce.

Old-Time "Flat Cakes"

- 2 cups sour milk *or* buttermilk
- 1 cup sour cream
- 3 teaspoons soda
- 2 eggs
- 1 teaspoon cinnamon

Enough flour to make a soft dough

Drop by tablespoon in hot oil, 365°. Then roll in cinnamon and sugar.

◆ MAUDIE'S MUSINGS ◆

WE ARE licensed as a restaurant, and the state inspector drops by from time to time to check us out. So far we have stayed good friends with him—no problems.

I like to see our guests eat...if they don't eat a lot, then I think maybe it wasn't good. I have a variety of pies for dessert, and folks are welcome to two or three pieces if they like.